SUCCESS STORIES FROM THE FRONTLINE

SUCCESS STORIES
from the Frontline

Intellectual Disabilities and Mental Health

*An anthology of first person stories
as submitted by patients and their families*

Edited by Madeline Hombert

Foreword and summaries by
Dr. Robin Friedlander, Psychiatrist MB, ChB M.Med (Psych), F.F. Psych (SA), FRCPC
and Tina Donnelly, RPN, BHSc

Success Stories from the Frontline: Intellectual Disabilities and Mental Health
Copyright© 2006 Robin Friedlander, Tina Donnelly, Madeline Hombert

First Edition October 2006

Friedlander/Donnelly Publishers
#207, 2248 Elgin Avenue
Port Coquitlam, BC
Canada V3C 2B2

LIBRARY AND ARCHIVES CANADA CATALOGUING IN PUBLICATION

Success stories from the frontline: intellectual disabilities and mental health: an anthology of first person stories as submitted by patients and their families / edited by Madeline Hombert; foreword and summaries by Robin Friedlander and Tina Donnelly.

Includes index.
ISBN 10: 0-9781467-0-0
ISBN 13: 978-0-9781467-0-2

1. People with mental disabilities—British Columbia—Interviews. 2. Mentally ill—British Columbia—Interviews. 3. Families of the mentally ill—British Columbia—Interviews. 4. People with mental disabilities—Mental health—British Columbia. I. Hombert, Madeline, 1944- II. Friedlander, Robin, 1954- III. Donnelly, Tina, 1952-

RC451.4.M47S88 2006   362.2092¢2711   C2006-904231-4

Design and layout by the Vancouver Desktop Publishing Centre
Printed in Canada by Ray Hignell Services Ltd.

This book is dedicated to the courageous individuals whose stories are told on these pages; to the families, caregivers and outreach workers who support them on a daily basis; and to all the other individuals who face each day with the dual challenges of developmental disability and mental illness.

The publishers wish to thank

Habiba Hemani at Astra Zeneca for the financial assistance that enabled us to embark on this project.

Tammy Lemercier for ensuring that the work was completed on time.

Holly Besmargian for office backup whenever we needed her.

Fraser Health for the resources and support to enable us to complete this important project.

Marie Nightingale for providing her support in advertising this valuable book of individual experiences.

Cheryl Head for proofreading the manuscript.

Riia Talve whose art has helped her express her feelings and whose gift has added so much to these pages.

And, most important,

Each individual and family whose honesty and sharing will serve to help others.

—*RF/TD/MH*

CONTENTS

FOREWORD

This book is about the group of people in our society who have the highest needs and yet who are the least served. It is about the people who fall through the proverbial "cracks" in the government system. On one side of the crack is the wide array of services developed for people in British Columbia with serious mental health needs such as schizophrenia and Bipolar mood disorders. On the other side is another array of services and supports for individuals in BC with intellectual disabilities (ID).

The term "ID" is used to refer to the 2%–3% of the population who are observed in childhood to have developmental delays such as late development of speech and/or difficulties with academics. As adults, these people would demonstrate associated difficulties in adaptive functioning such as using money or public transport. Although the cause of the ID is often unknown in about half the cases, a genetic syndrome or other identifiable cause may be demonstrated. Overall, IQ testing shows a score of less than 70. Even so, such individuals may have and often do have unique strengths. As examples, it is accepted that people with Williams Syndrome have perfect pitch/musicality and some individuals with autism have savant skills in math.

This book is concerned with those individuals who have both ID and serious mental illness. This is more common than would be expected by chance.

Just less than 1% of the population in Canada receives government supports because of ID and about 3% of the general population has serious mental health needs. People with ID have a 30%–40% risk of concurrent mental disorder and a 10% rate of serious mental illness such as schizophrenia or bipolar. In other words, for each person receiving government services for having ID, the chance for concurrent mental illness is three times the expected rate in the general population! These are the very people who are being neglected by current government agencies; the highest needs people who, through no fault of their own, have been pushed into the "cracks" of the system.

That is the nature of government. Government services are established because of recognized public needs. Those needs are generally identified in western countries by powerful lobby groups. In Canada there has been successful advocacy to get adequately government funded services for those people diagnosed with ID and another set of services for those diagnosed with mental illness. Services for the two distinct groups are provided by two separate support agencies.

There remains the third group – the people with both ID and mental illness. This group stands alone.

There never is enough money available for all public services. When any specific agency or ministry department does receive funding approval, the mandate becomes restricted in order to ensure that the group is adequately resourced. There is no room in the budgets of the established agencies to provide add-on services to a special group of higher needs citizens. Because this new third group does not have its own powerful advocates, it does not always appear on the radar screens of decision makers. It falls in those darn "cracks."

We generally use the term "Dual Diagnosis" to label this third group, but, in BC where we live and work, the term has been co-opted by the substance abuse lobby to refer to individuals who are addicted with substance abuse and who also have concurrent mental illness. Because of this situation, in this book, we will use the term IDMH to refer to those with both intellectual disabilities and problems with mental health.

That is what this book is about: our work with "the other dual diagnosis", our work with the special group of people and families whose needs too often fall through the frustrating cracks in the system.

Success is often defined as the accomplishment of an aim.

Our aim was to identify individuals with IDMH who were assisted by a community mental health team over a period of years and to give them a voice to describe the combined experience of both ID and mental illness.

Previously, the BC Association for Community Living (BCACL), a powerful advocacy group in BC for individuals with ID, published a series of stories highlighting successful transition from institution to community living. As well, the Canadian Mental Health Association (CMHA) in BC published an anthology of personal stories documenting people's struggles with serious mental illness and into recovery. Neither publication recorded stories of individuals with IDMH, or the experiences of their families.

This book not only identifies the neglected "third group" but also gives these individuals and families their voice. These intimate stories were written by the people who can convey the message better than anyone else. Who better to tell the story of recovery than those who have lived the experience?

We first recognized the power of personal stories when we hosted the panel presentation of families and individuals with IDMH at the NADD conference held in Vancouver. We (the clinicians) were brought to tears by hearing about the steps that made positive differences in the lives of these special people.

When the concurrent mental illness initially appeared, neither the families nor the individuals concerned had any idea of what was happening. As all the literature and family support resources (on schizophrenia, for example) referred to individuals with typical intellectual functioning, they had no idea of how long and difficult the road ahead would be.

This book can not be faulted for having a "hidden agenda", as the message is clear and explicit. It comes at a critical time for health planning and for funding decisions. It is delivered through these personal stories and is wrapped in hope.

Although unique in BC, this really is an international issue as countries all over the world must deal with a new generation of children and adults with ID living outside of institutions and in the community.

Our message of hope is that the policy/decision makers in the Ministries of Social Services and Mental Health in British Columbia will recognize the needs of this unique group. Our managers in the Regional Health Authorities have been made aware of this population and there is an attempt to address this need.

There are, however, other systems in BC who also need to be involved including CLBC (Community Living BC), the government crown agency responsible for children and adults with ID and the Provincial Health Services Authority.

This is a call for these agencies to pay closer attention to this group of individuals; there is a need to work together at a provincial level to develop dedicated cross systems planning and funding for this high needs population.

—*Robin/Tina*

OUR STORIES

AMBER

Amber is now in her late 20's.

Recent genetic testing demonstrated that she has a deletion on one of her chromosomes (9p-) which is extremely rare. The family has connected with other families in North America who have children showing the same chromosomal deletion.

Amber's mood and anxiety symptoms were severe and debilitating. They did not respond predictably to conventional psychiatric interventions such as medication, behavioral supports, family support, art therapy or hospitalization.

It is unknown if her atypical response to treatment is related to her genetic syndrome.

Amber has a loving family but they simply do not have the energy to deal with another extreme episode. Her social worker is committed to completing the arrangements for Amber's move to a supported living home before his impending retirement.

—RF

AMBER'S STORY

Amber's life began with difficulty.

At three months, my pregnancy became fragile but it proceeded until almost 29 weeks when our tiny (3lb.5oz) baby girl was born. The complicated breech birth left her with respiratory distress, jaundice, lethargy, a cardiac murmur, intracranial bleeding and a poor sucking reflex. Blood transfusions were required and Amber spent her first two months in an isolet in the Intensive Care nursery. (Visiting with friends the next day, my husband looked at their coffee pot and said "my baby daughter is smaller than that.")

Once at home, Amber still had sucking problems and took an unusually long time to take her bottles. Doctors tried to reassure us by saying "she's premature, she'll catch up."

At a year old, Amber was diagnosed with mild cerebral palsy and the pediatrician enrolled her in an infant development program. Home physiotherapy helped Amber to begin sitting up within a couple of months and this was followed with two days a week in group therapy. When she was two and a half, we cried with joy when she started walking. By the time she was four, she was speaking. Fine motor skills remained a major hurdle, even with occupational therapy.

Elementary school years were passed in a special needs classroom and high school was achieved within the structure of life skills programs. Although Amber did not learn to read words, she did learn to appreciate pictures and illustrations in books and she still enjoys this pastime. Although she did not learn to write, she did learn to print her own name. Her graduation was an emotional moment for everyone.

When Amber was young, she had re-occurring upper respiratory infections, ear infections and Bronchitis. In the years 1981–1990, tubes were inserted in her ears to help the fluid buildup and her adenoids were removed. The ear wax buildup continues to this day. Her nose was cauterized about ten years ago to help stem frequent nose bleeds and had to be cauterized again in 2004.

At just ten years old, Amber began menstruating. She was prescribed Minovral from 1993–1998 for excessive bleeding. Contradictory to her early onset of puberty, Amber didn't get chicken pox, normally experienced by young children, until she was 19 years old.

At age 13, still bedwetting, the doctor did a urine test and found the presence of sugar. After a few days of intensive in-hospital testing, the diagnosis was Type II Diabetes. This was initially controlled by diet and exercise and then with Novo-glybride pills. Today she is on Metformin.

Each year Amber has her eyes checked by a doctor that specializes in Ocular Diabetes. (And each year the doctor comments on her beautifully arched eyebrows!)

Years of medication have left Amber's teeth permanently stained. She wore braces for years and now has a permanent retainer behind her top front teeth. Her wisdom teeth were extracted in 1999. As she is terrified of needles, all her dental work is performed under general anesthetic.

Her feet are long, flat and narrow (8 ½ AAAAA). When she started walking, the Orthopedic Specialist said "Her feet work for her. Why should we put her through surgery if it would only be cosmetic?" Shoe shopping is a challenge and she sees a Diabetic Foot Care Podiatrist every five weeks. Her fingers are fine boned and elongated and when she is under stress, she picks at and pulls her fingernails and toenails as far down as she can.

Despite having Scoliosis, Amber enrolled in the disabled riding program and added this experience to her list of accomplishments. Once again, the whole family was reduced to tears as we watched her sitting tall on a horse, enjoying every moment.

Just as things seemed to be under control and her learning disabilities were acknowledged and managed, Amber was challenged yet again.

Changes began happening when school life ended. With the departure from the structure of daily attendance and work activity with peers, there was nothing to stimulate Amber on a daily basis. It was six months before she could begin attending a day program on even a twice-weekly basis. At this point, her home changed as well. Our family moved out of a three bedroom house with a familiar yard and into a two bedroom townhouse with no yard.

At first, Amber became unusually quiet. Then she became very anxious and unhappy. This was very different from the behavior and personality that had been reflected throughout her life. Fortunately her regular physician recognized the new problem.

Amber was referred to a Psychiatrist and in March 1998, she was diagnosed with depression. She was initially treated with Paxil. This drug was replaced with Luvox, which, unfortunately, caused severe obsessing over the weather combined with a drug induced mania. She was hospitalized for a month to safely remove all medications, and then was started on a regime of Nortriptyline and Clonazepam. The resulting months showed such improvement that, by the end of 2001, all medications were discontinued.

In December 2003, for seemingly unknown reasons, Amber had a relapse. Her depression worsened and in May 2004 she resumed taking Clonazepam. Olanzapine was added late that year but then was stopped due to weight gain.

Other medications were also tried including Seroquel, Lorazepam, Divalproex and another trial of Nortriptyline. Although the latter seemed to have some positive results it was discontinued due to frequent urine infections and constipation. The majority of medications prescribed would begin to help Amber but then their effectiveness would wear off. Life would become a test of tolerance for everyone.

At this time, June of 2006, Amber is still experiencing sudden mood swings and anxieties and she still obsesses over the weather. Our family and her doctor are working hard to try and get back the "Happy Amber" but it is a frustrating journey.

Changes continue to cause great stress so everyone works to keep Amber's life structured around a well-balanced routine. She attends a social program five days a week which she really enjoys. The staff members comment on her great sense of humor and contagious giggle. When she is "Happy Amber" life is wonderful. She loves animals, listening to music, playing her video games and playing games on the computer. Weekend visits to the shopping mall, buying coloring books and visiting the animals in the pet stores are her most enjoyable activities.

Amber began her life fighting for her very existence and she still shows this resiliency. In spite of the dual challenges she has faced and continues to face, Amber forges ahead and optimistically cooperates with every form of treatment or therapy that may help her along her path. She has been fortunate to have been correctly diagnosed, to be surrounded by a supportive and loving family and to have caring, dedicated professionals available to assist with her progress.

Added note: In order to find a name for Amber's state of health, the whole family (mother, father, Amber and her sister) underwent genetics testing. No hereditary or genetic abnormalities were discovered. The geneticist pronounced that Amber ". . . has a syndrome or collection of physical anomalies and it may take time until it is identified." When he was asked why this diagnosis hadn't been made twenty years prior, his response was forthright and obvious: "20 years ago testing was black and white, today it is color."

STEPHANIE

Stephanie is in her early twenties. She lives at home with her parents and with the assistance of a full-time caregiver.

She was identified in early childhood with a rare genetic syndrome (Aicardi syndrome) which caused profound intellectual disability, lack of speech and daily seizures. In spite of the handicaps, the first 13 years of her life went smoothly and were free from behavioral problems. Stephanie's home, school and recreational life were full and happy.

Then puberty arrived! Stephanie became distressed for no predictable reason and, when upset, would lash out violently or scream incessantly. As she could not verbalize any pain or reason for distress, the clinician's job was akin to that of a detective, looking at all possibilities with her parents and support people being witnesses.

—RF

STEPHANIE'S STORY

Stephanie was born in August 1983. Full term. No complications. An 18 year old unmarried young woman gave birth but I am her mother. She will always be daddy's little girl and mommy's baby no matter how many years pass.

At three months Stephanie began having infantile febrile seizures. What started one day as a single episode (her tiny face turning red and her bending over with clenched fists as if she were having a bowel movement) escalated within 4 days to non-stop convulsions. She was rushed to emergency and after a month of in-hospital testing and observing, we learned that she had Aicardi Syndrome, an extremely rare disorder caused when the corpus collusum doesn't form during development. There were other little problems in her brain discovered by CT Scan but the bottom line was Severe Mental Impairment, Substantial Physical Disabilities, and Epilepsy. With the less than 400 cases known worldwide, at least 75% of the Aicardi girls (the syndrome is unique to females) died within their first two years, and more than half of those remaining perished before they were four. Stephanie wasn't given much hope at all.

After we dealt with the initial shock and grief, we just decided to carry on and take one day at a time. We treated Stephanie just as we would have treated her if she had been born without limitations. She traveled to Europe, Disneyland, Hawaii, across Canada by train, ferry, car and plane. She went to a special preschool and kindergarten and shocked all her specialists when she suddenly stood up one day and walked. She wasn't supposed to be able to do that at all. Only 2 others in the world with the same syndrome could walk! She may not have been able to speak but she could sure smile her way around anyone and she could—and still can—indicate her pleasure, wishes, displeasure, anger by the strength of her handclapping. She did not learn to bite or chew food but she can gulp down a malted milk or thick milkshake as fast as any teenager.

From age 1 to age 12 she stoically underwent at least six major surgeries or invasive procedures to correct orthopedic problems or other issues. As well, during each year of her young life, she had at least two hospital stays of periods of 2 to 6 days, many of these visits in life-threatening situations. (Every parent of a chronically ill child or a seriously disabled child has experienced the feeling of almost-uncomfortable familiarity when nursing staff and emergency personnel address you by your first name!)

For thirteen years Stephanie went to bed at 7:30 pm and awoke at 7:30 am like clockwork. No music or vacuum cleaner or loud conversation would make any difference. One smile, one hug, ten minutes of "Yanni"'s new age music and she would be out like a light. She attended school helped by a one-to-one aide and she participated in many after-school activities at a special program.

Then our world started to crumble. It began just after puberty.

Menstruation wasn't really a big problem at first because she wore diapers. It was just a case of more frequent changes being necessary. Her seizures began to worsen a week before her period, however, and her moods changed drastically. She would be very angry and would display her discomfort. About this time, she also seemed to be developing more intellectual awareness. This was good in one way, but bad in another. As Stephanie realized that she couldn't communicate with us, she became angrier. She had been keeping her diaper dry all day with the constant attention of both her caregivers and us. If we took her to the bathroom every 2 hours, she would perform and be so proud of herself. But, if she had an "accident", she would get upset and scream at being wet. The menstrual fluids didn't exactly fit within this two-hour system and she would be furious at being wet/dirty. When I changed her, she would pull my hair and lash out at me for not catching this "little problem".

For two years this situation became worse and worse and we began to see such sadness in her eyes. We thought she was having headaches or some other pain but the neurologists disagreed. They moved her Epival up and then down, thinking it was the dosage of drug causing mood disorders. They also felt it was Stephanie's sensing an impending seizure that caused her screaming episodes. More anti-seizure drugs were added to the point of Stephanie having very little of her original alertness. Her sleep (and ours) was interrupted 3 to 4 times each and every night. Sometimes she would go back to sleep, sometimes she would not. We took turns having night duty – my husband let me sleep on weekends and I let him sleep during the week. Stephanie continued to have episodes of extreme anger alternating with sadness.

An ob-gyn began giving Stephanie Depo-Provera shots every 3 months. This stopped her periods and this solved one anxiety for Stephanie. It did not stop the obvious pain she was having and we began to see a terrible change in her personality. She could be smiling one minute and screaming wildly the next. Extreme behavior included pulling hair and scratching anyone around her or rubbing her own hands until they bled. When she was having a bad time, her seizures went totally out of control as well.

When my eldest son was killed in a work-related accident, it truly seemed as if our family had been selected for some Supreme Being's endurance test. Traveling together to Alberta to help with arrangements wasn't possible. Qualified, experienced care for Stephanie was only available for minimal days. I went right away but my husband had to follow three days later for the actual funeral. (People who are able to depend on a neighbor or regular babysitter sometimes have no concept of the difficulties some families have to arrange appropriate child care! Even if funding is available, the bigger problem is finding an appropriate person to hire!)

We moved across the street from the high school when Stephanie was 13. If she had a particularly bad seizure, or a nosebleed, or wouldn't stop crying, I could walk over and bring her home. The teachers in the life skills class were very understanding to our situation and they allowed me to bring her to school late if she had a seizure upon waking and needed a short nap. When she turned 18, we were able to extend Stephanie's school attendance by one year, but we really didn't know what we would do once she was out of the school system. Stephanie didn't have enough abilities to fit within a work program or even most of the group activities at other day programs.

Although we had approval for 10 days of respite a year, we didn't have anyone to call for relief. For over five years, we had no rest at all. We couldn't even take Stephanie on a holiday with us any more. She had developed an inner ear problem so severe she could not fly or tolerate extreme temperatures. She tired easily so a long trip by car wasn't an option and her screaming did not make us good candidates for motels or hotels. Her physical strength and manic outbursts resulted in my being hospitalized three times in five years for emergency hernia surgeries and a wrist replacement. My husband was our only constant companion and he remained steadfast—taking Stephanie for car rides and malted milk treats on weekends while I recouped my strength.

Finally, two wondrous things happened.

First, the ObGyn applied to the hospital board for approval for Stephanie to have a hysterectomy. Once she met Stephanie a few times, she agreed that there had to be another problem, one that was causing Stephanie much distress. The hospital policy required further medical intervention for at least a year but the process was at least started.

Second, the neurologist was changed and subsequently we were referred to Dr. Friedlander at the children's hospital psychiatric unit. It took just a couple of visits for us to learn that Stephanie was now suffering from a deep case of depression.

Remember the "good news" and "bad news"? It still remained true. Stephanie's intelligence and cognizance of her condition had increased enough that she now hated her seizures, hated her inability to speak and hated the pain she was enduring on a daily basis. Who wouldn't be depressed?!

The state of affairs was bad enough that we had no option but to agree to two months of hospitalization for assessment. The Ministry provided funding for 24 hour care on a one-to-one basis in hospital and, painfully for all concerned, we stayed away for the first week. Anti-depressants were begun and, with some "tweaking" of dosage over a few months, we saw an enormous change. Stephanie's smiles were returning and her compulsive hand-rubbing had virtually disappeared. The hot and ugly plastic protective "mitt" she had worn for three years was thrown away!

After a year, the hospital board approved her hysterectomy and Stephanie had her surgery when she was 20. Not surprising, they discovered that she had misshapen, darkened ovaries and a uterus full of all sorts of fibrous tissues. Our ObGyn told us that, due to the condition of her organs, Stephanie must have been suffering an intolerable amount of pain each and every month! The ovaries were tested for cancer but, thankfully, everything was benign and she began a regime of low-dose hormone replacement therapy.

With the pain gone, and the antidepressants doing their job, we had our girl back. She returned to going to bed at 8 and sleeping through the night. Mom and dad got a full 8 hours of sleep each night and romance returned to the marriage. Mom lost weight and her complexion cleared up. Dad started humming in the shower. When Dr. Friedlander transferred us to the Fraser Valley Mental Health Clinic (still under his care) for bi-monthly, and then quarterly visits, people commented on the change in everyone.

Things weren't all a bed of roses. Stephanie was out of school and got bored very easily. I had turned 60 (gasp!) and I just couldn't keep up the pace any more. We could only get approval for 3 days per week of a day program and that just wasn't suitable. The program was 9:30 am until 3 pm. If Stephanie slept in a bit or dawdled over breakfast, sometimes they wouldn't leave the house until 10:30 or later and it wasn't unusual for them to be back by 2:35. If I had to see my own doctor, I had to get an appointment on one of only 3 days a week available, and only between noon and 1:30 to ensure I could be back home through city traffic in time for Stephanie's return. Some of the support workers were wonderful and some were just plain useless to all concerned. Stephanie deserved better.

Again we had divine intervention through a social worker who knew her way around the system, and also spent the time to listen to us and make observations about what would/could really make a difference. We all agreed that we had to find a way to make the financial support of the government go further. We drew up a plan that we felt would make life good for Stephanie. This included recreation, support, playtimes and friends. We made a list of what it would take to make this plan a reality and what the implementation would cost. For our family, the solution was to have an experienced caregiver living with us so that the hours could be flexible. As our home is a modest one, we knew we needed more room. Stephanie's social worker told us about a fund that covered "one time" needs and we started the application process.

We formed a microboard, establishing a private "Society" with the singular purpose of "supporting a person with physical and developmental needs by providing living, recreation and social assistance". This cost $100. Then we set up a budget and applied for individualized funding through the new society.

One requirement was that we could prove that we could hire a live-in caregiver for 5 days a week, 8 hours a day, for less cost of the day program that was providing only three "6 hour" days per week. We added in the cost of providing respite for our ten existing days and the cost of the 4-hour per week of community activities. There were other odds and ends to consider such as insurance and Workers Compensation and holidays but even adding everything to the list, the cost for our new society to provide MORE support for Stephanie at LESS cost to the ministry was obvious. The bonus to this was the fact that, should we ever move to another area, the funding would go with us. For once we would not have to re-apply according to any guidelines established by a different municipality or city.

We applied for the special funding and received enough to help us add on a bedroom, bathroom and playroom. A few weeks before the renovations were completed; we applied to an agency ("Able Nannies") that specializes in caregivers and nannies that have specific training and experience in working with either physically or mentally challenged people. Exactly a year ago, we welcomed our new family member to our home and life has gone from darn good to just plain wonderful!

Stephanie gets up with a smile whenever she feels like it and her friend, our wonderful Jonally, is there with a hug, a hot bubble bath and breakfast. They go to the park in the morning and return for lunch. They play in their little playroom with toys and music or watch TV and it brings tears to my eyes to peek in and see Stephanie sitting on the floor and humming "almost" in tune to music videos. Her intelligence and awareness seem to have jumped a notch in the past year as well, perhaps because of her contentment and the total commitment of her nanny. She loves country music, especially Faith Hill, and just last week amazed us all when she grabbed a celebrity magazine and kissed a small black and white photo of her singing idol.

In the afternoon, the two girls go to another park where Stephanie can enjoy a wading pool and fountains or they go for a car ride. Sundays Stephanie goes swimming or riding the carousel with another special person. They also go to White Rock to walk along the pier or at the mall where she sees her many favorite "old folks". These understanding seniors now look for her each Sunday. They smile at her and she smiles right back, often adding a hug!

With all this assistance in place, my husband and I look forward to spending our evenings and Saturdays with our little "Sweet Baboo". Stephanie continues to have a regular 8 pm bedtime and she sleeps through the night ninety percent of the time. We are all healthier for this change.

Because nanny's family is far way in the Philippines, she is happy to earn overtime occasionally. My husband and I have actually been able to slip away for little weekend holidays a few times. When we do go, we are totally at ease knowing Stephanie is safe at home in the care of someone who knows her and loves her. Sometimes the four of us pack up for a short road trip or a fun adventure like going to the go-kart track!

Stephanie still endures her seizures but the extended "Grand Mal" type that last 15 to 20 minutes seem to be occurring just once a week. The smaller ones occur just once a day and she laughs those off if we cuddle her and say "Dammit—the uh-oh's are back!" How different this is from a few years ago when even the smallest seizure would make her either furious or extremely sad—or both.

Our last visit to see Dr. Friedlander was another positive reflection of the success of the previous years. We now are on a "call if required" basis and are officially off the books at the clinic.

Stephanie is 23 now. To our knowledge, she is the third-eldest surviving girl with Aicardi Syndrome in the world. She wasn't supposed to sit up. She did. She wasn't supposed to walk. She did. She wasn't supposed to live past childhood. She did. We had waited over two years to adopt a perfect little girl and it turned out that we got the little girl who was perfect for us.

Stephanie isn't a bona fide teacher but she has taught everyone in her world that, with perseverance and love and commitment, there is absolutely nothing that cannot be overcome. She has shown us all that we each have strengths that we didn't know we possessed.

Our family will ever be thankful that both our neurologist and our pediatrician cared more for our daughter than for their own egos and generously referred us to another doctor, one who could see the one unique tree in the forest.

Success is a relative term. For some people it may seem strange to consider a life of seizures or an ongoing need for medication and psychiatric monitoring as being successful. For families who have spent years without any progress and, worse, without any hope for improvement and/or without anyone who seemed to truly care for their children, just the fact that appropriate support is available is a success. Just the fact that the problem has been identified has been a success. Just the fact that we are surviving is a success.

We hope our family's example will be one more recorded statement to prove the need for additional funding for the dual diagnosis clinics and one more beacon of hope for other parents in their pursuit of a better life.

DEEPA

Deepa is now in her early 20's and is a beloved member of an immigrant family. As a result of childhood meningitis, she was left with developmental delay and seizures. Her parents have always provided a safe, nurturing home for Deepa. Their only concern is her slowed rate of learning.

When Deepa was in her teens and attending a special education life skills class, she began to wrongly believe that people were staring at her. When this paranoia evolved into seriously aggressive behavior, her observant and concerned teacher suggested that her parents get a referral to the Mental Health team.

—RF

DEEPA'S STORY

After an episode of meningitis when she was just 8 months old, our daughter began to have seizures. The doctor prescribed a daily dose of Tegretol to suppress them. As she grew, her development seemed slow and, after many tests and consultations with specialists, it was concluded that our sweet child would never function at a high level of intelligence. Nonetheless, she was learning at a regular pace and was a much loved little girl.

Childhood and puberty progressed without any problems and Deepa developed as a happy and cheerful person. Music was a favorite hobby during these years and Deepa was acknowledged as being a very good, attentive student at school. After school she spent her free time reading, writing, enjoying basketball and playing Nintendo games.

When Deepa was fifteen, there was noticeable weight gain and so the Tegretol was replaced by Topomax. Coincidentally, her life— and ours—began to change drastically soon after.

Deepa wandered around like a lost soul. It began with her losing interest in activities. She had no interest in her hobbies or games and she withdrew from family. The daughter who once loved to spend time with her mother and many close friends started to isolate herself. The child who once lit up our home with her smile now was a disruptive force for everyone. Her sadness was like a dark cloud around her and we could do nothing to help her.

Soon, Deepa's sleep patterns changed. Many nights she would not go to sleep at all. Even worse, when she could not sleep, she would go from room to room turning on all the lights, and insist that everyone stay awake with her. Her anger grew daily. We knew that she was suffering from some mental illness and we also knew we were all suffering with her.

Then she started misbehaving at school, at first just speaking badly about her classmates to her teacher. This progressed to actually attacking both the teacher and other students. Many times this behavior resulted in her dismissal from school. Within a short period of three months, Deepa had changed from a popular student to an angry, disruptive problem.

After a few months without improvement, Deepa's teacher met with us. She agreed that there had to be a medical explanation for this drastic change and she suggested that we make an appointment with a child psychiatrist whose opinion she highly valued.

Fortunately, we were able to meet with the psychiatrist without much delay. The initial consultations were intense—every two weeks for six months—and Deepa began a closely-monitored regime of medication. Within a week she returned to her regular sleep patterns. It wasn't long before we saw changes in her attitude and behavior. She was still aggressive and angry but at least we were sleeping. We were no longer exhausted and we could deal with her problems much better.

The consultations at the clinic office continued on a less frequent basis for another six months and then Deepa began a program known as CBI. After another 18 months of this therapy, we could see a marked improvement, perhaps as much as 80%!

As this book is being written, Deepa is doing very well. She has returned to being a happy person. She has resumed interest in her daily activities and is always smiling. She attends a day program and after 21 months in that program, we have not had one complaint about her behavior. At home she makes her own breakfast, does her own laundry and helps her mom with preparing meals. She gets along with everyone she knows, and she has even returned to making jokes and to being the wonderful, happy daughter we knew in the first 15 years of her life.

There is no argument that the years between age 15 and 20 were a nightmare. Deepa's mother took the brunt of the daily physical punishment and it is a wonder that she did not break down completely. Although I did my best to intervene in the aggressive assaults, my wife endured so much and my life was one of worry for both her and Deepa. Thankfully, this has all changed and we all have returned to living in a happier home.

Any disability brings challenges. An added diagnosis can be overwhelming and can destroy individuals. Patience is very important and persistence in seeking help is absolutely necessary. No one can deal with these issues alone and our family is living proof of the positive results of having access to both a highly-skilled doctor and a professional, capable mental health team.

ELIZABETH

Elizabeth is now in her mid-fifties.

From an early age, she was noted to have an autism spectrum disorder in association with her intellectual disability and seizures. Elizabeth grew up in the period when care for people with ID was changing from an institutional model to a new paradigm called community living. Elizabeth has experienced both models and her father graphically describes his encounters with the changing system of care.

In her adult life, Elizabeth first presented with annual bouts of picking at her skin, digging inside herself, inappropriate disrobing and disruptive screaming. This was ultimately assessed to be a masked presentation of depression but, in fact, she has a triple psychiatric diagnosis (intellectual disability, autism and depression). Elizabeth is fortunate to reside in an above-average, stable group home. She is further supported by regular visits from her doting father.

—RF

ELIZABETH'S STORY.

Elizabeth is the third child of a military family. She was conceived within an environment of a heavy radar system which emitted 200 megawatts of pulsed power every 90 seconds as its antenna continuously rotated 360 degrees. The entire pregnancy was experienced in these conditions 24 hours a day. There is evidence that there was also fine electronic spray similar to ocean spray in the immediate vicinity of the antenna. A colleague working under the same conditions in another location also became the father of a similarly affected child. A cousin who practices in the field of medicine in the US conducted an exhaustive search of family records which revealed no other incidence of mental disability. Although these background facts do not prove any certainty, they are noted because it remains my belief that there may be a connection between the continuous exposure to massive electromagnetic radiation and Elizabeth's diagnosis.

Elizabeth's story covers four relevant periods between 1956 and 2006 and it includes changing terminology. What began as "mental retardation" evolved into "mentally handicapped", "mentally challenged" and "developmentally disabled." The following reflects these changes.

PERIOD 1: 1956 – 1959

At age 7 months, Elizabeth went to her first Christmas party. There were about 100 people attending which included numerous excited and rowdy children. This added to the general noise and holiday music. Elizabeth reacted with horror and screamed so much that we immediately took her home. This reaction was the first sign of her total aversion to crowds.

Her physical development seemed average. She walked, sat up, and began her first words at the usual stages of infancy. When I fed her lunch, she said "mom-mom", "all gone" and then "Bye-Bye" when I returned to work.

Just before Elizabeth's second birthday, she was standing in her crib and suddenly began having massive convulsions. The seizures continued as we rushed to the local nursing station. We were redirected fifteen miles away to a community hospital where the doctors immediately sent us another 60 miles down the highway to a children's hospital. After thorough examinations by many specialists, we received the diagnosis of "profound mental retardation—cause unknown". Although we were advised to place her in an institution where she could receive extensive support, we chose to take our daughter home and dedicate ourselves to her care. Her seizures were monitored through frequent visits back to the hospital. Things were managed reasonably well until the family situation changed.

I received a promotion that demanded a move to a new city. The family was a transient, military family dropped into an established community. This was the '50's and the older siblings were often ridiculed for having a "weird kid" for a sister. As my new position required a great deal of international travel with many long periods away from home, my wife had to manage most of the parenting duties and Elizabeth's constant needs were almost overwhelming.

There was no choice but to place Elizabeth in a Hospital School (Institution for the Mentally Handicapped).

PERIOD 2: 1959-1968

The 30 mile trip to the institution was very emotionally painful and the abrupt reception was worse. Upon arrival, the doctor and charge nurses took Elizabeth and warned us to ". . . not come back for six weeks so she can adjust. If you come back before then, you'll be taking her back home with you."

After six weeks, we went for our first visit. When we embarked on a car ride, formerly her special delight, Elizabeth seemed to be absolutely confused. She did not seem to know who these "strangers" were, or why they were with her. It took several attempts but eventually she started to enjoy the outings in the car again. Soon we tried adding visits to restaurants but when Elizabeth reacted to the other customers with loud screaming, this was abandoned in favor of take-out fare or food from home. (The new arrangement became a favorite treat and the car seat picnics, especially after ordering from drive through windows, continue to this day.)

Eventually, a routine evolved where Elizabeth would spend one full week each month at home. In addition, every three weeks my wife and I would spend a weekend near the institution so we could maximize her car rides and personal attention.

Although we never actually saw regular activities within her hospital setting, it appeared that Elizabeth was clearly benefiting from the institutional regime. The staff understood Elizabeth's resistance to any change as well as her requirement for predictability and they followed a rigid routine with her. As time went on, it became clear that she had become a ward favorite. Although she preferred separation from other patients, she was not aggressive towards anyone and she seemed happy. As she grew, she became a "contented loner". (This is a family trait on both sides.)

In 1966, I was transferred again, this time thousands of miles away to the West Coast. Unfortunately, the nearest residential institution was no longer accepting new admissions as the government was changing to a new model of housing called "Community Living". Elizabeth had to remain in Ontario while we fought the system. Thanks to the persistence of the military social worker, a loophole was found. The institution could accept a transfer or exchange of patients from elsewhere in Canada. This solution turned out to be more difficult than first suspected. It was two years before a family that would agree to transfer their child to another province was found. This was accomplished quite by accident when our same dedicated social worker met a world-traveling, seaborne couple moored nearby. As this couple had chosen to have virtually no contact with their two committed children, it was no concern for them to have one child sent across the country. Their only request was that all the paperwork and even the actual accompaniment of their child was handled without their involvement.

We were more than happy to comply with everything to get our daughter closer to home and so we began the paperwork in earnest.

During this time, our family had been going through other difficulties. My father-in-law had developed Alzheimer's and it became necessary for my wife to live in Vancouver to care for his daily needs. As a senior officer, I had responsibilities that required me to remain at my post on the military base all week but I was able to commute to Vancouver most weekends.

It was very important to keep my family as close-knit as possible and to give my wife the support she needed. All the while, the intense negotiations to transfer Elizabeth to the West Coast remained in the forefront.

Just as the plans to transfer Elizabeth were being finalized, our family was dealt a blow. I suffered a serious heart attack.

Thankfully, Elizabeth's older sister was available to take over. She assumed the dual challenges of first traveling East with an unfamiliar companion and his caregiver and then of making the return trip to the West Coast with her sister. Elizabeth thoroughly enjoyed the plane ride to Vancouver, giggling joyfully and expressing sheer delight in periods of air turbulence. The trip proved to be a bonding experience for both of them and they have remained very close ever since. No matter how long they are separated physically, Elizabeth always enthusiastically and lovingly greets her sister at each visit.

PERIOD 3: 1968-1988

After a few days with the family at her grandfather's home, Elizabeth was admitted to the residential hospital/school where the staff ratio seemed to be 1 to 10. Neither her sleeping arrangements nor her daily activity on the ward were ever made available for review. For parental visits, staff would simply bring a patient to the main door for pickup. Our times together would consist of either a long car ride on weekends or a trip home to spend a full week with us. The latter was a true labor of love as it would leave everyone exhausted. The return to the residence never varied: ring the buzzer, watch staff usher Elizabeth inside, and then be dismissed swiftly but courteously.

Elizabeth's records clearly document her continued dislike of crowds. (A crowd for Elizabeth means there is more than one person present). In the hospital general assembly room, she would invariably seek out empty space for privacy. Elizabeth's passiveness made her an easy target for more hyperactive residents. She has been left with permanent scars from one particular incident when an agitated individual ran sharp fingernails down both of her arms. Other unwelcome approaches from residents led to Elizabeth developing biting as a self-defense mechanism. Still another legacy from the residence is the enduring habit of sleeping with her head fully under bedcovers. (The hospital left all the lights on in the wards, including sleeping areas, 24 hours a day.)

There were some options available for her development but it took several years before she could be persuaded to join even kitchen skills training. When she did, Elizabeth was finally able to gain some independence and social skills. She could be trusted to go unaccompanied to another building on-site to attend the course and to return promptly. Unfortunately, a serious fire occurred in the kitchen, the course was ended and Elizabeth suffered a setback.

Soon after, Elizabeth moved to a smaller ward with about half of her original ward co-residents. New policies made families more welcome and we were invited to several meetings, birthday parties and Christmas events. The new arrangement felt like a more "homey" surrounding. In spite of these improvements, Elizabeth still sought access to unoccupied space so she could be alone. The staff did their very best to meet her basic requirements and we continued the monthly routine—one week at the family home and two weeks later, car rides in the area for the day. Still a stickler for regimentation, even at home, Elizabeth insisted on sitting in one particular chair at the kitchen table. She also insisted on eating the same scrambled eggs and ham with tomatoes at each meal!! No substitutes please.

In the early '80's, the government announced formal closure of the facility. The intention was to place the residents from all provincial institutions into various community group homes. It was a "one-size-fits-all" approach and, in spite of protests, families were given no options. The major changes took place between 1986 and 1988 and Elizabeth's needs were still being monitored at the institution as late as November 1987.

At this period, Elizabeth was considered as being physically healthy in spite of minor problems such as eczema and hay fever. She was still considered to be epileptic but had not experienced seizures since infancy. Mentally, her autism was mainly reflected in resistance to change, intolerance of noise, and occasional extreme agitation. Statements from specialists over these years were similar and unanimous in the observation that Elizabeth needed care, supervision and protection on a one-to-one basis 24 hours a day and that any sudden changes to her routines be minimized.

With that information, primarily the need for constant supervision, it seemed ironic that a Ministry decision was made to place Elizabeth into a private corporation's group home. In spite of strenuous parental objection, Elizabeth was moved out of the institutional setting on an impartial predetermined date—a date that just happened to occur a mere 12 days after her mother died from a lengthy battle with cancer.

PERIOD 4: 1988 – 2006

The day Elizabeth moved into a split-level 3 bedroom home, she experienced:

- The loss of her familiar home
- The loss of familiar staff
- The loss of contact with familiar bed, residents and routine activity
- The grief from the loss of her mother 12 days earlier.

For an emotionally fragile person who can not cope with change even under the best of circumstances, the inflexibility of the moving date was especially unfortunate. Her move to the new community was ill-timed and seemingly carried out with gross insensitivity.

Although I was totally occupied with watching helplessly as my precious wife lay dying in the cancer control centre, I managed to maintain the weekly outings with my daughter. On Elizabeth's last visit to the palliative facility, she became frightened and tried to pull her mother out of the bed. When she couldn't get her to rise, she grabbed my arm, screamed at the top of her lungs, and pulled me away from the hospital. Just days after this experience, her life was totally uprooted. First, her beloved mother died. Then, after just two brief familiarization visits to the group home, she was quickly moved into it. For any autistic person dropped into a new environment with total strangers, the adjustment to drastically different procedures, even new food, must have been an absolute nightmare and Elizabeth couldn't even find comfort with her family.

Over fifteen years later, at precisely the same time of year, Elizabeth still suffers a great deal of distress. Her keen memory and deep emotional feelings were demonstrated on her first trip back to the family home after her mother's death. She knew something was wrong. Someone was missing. Intuitively, she went straight to the powder room and picked up the hairbrush mom used to re-arrange her hair on each home visit. She took the hairbrush with her when she left and literally carried it with her for 10 years—even to medical appointments!! This is a lady who had been categorized with an IQ measurement of well below 70! Since that visit, and on every week-end visit back home since then, Elizabeth continues to routinely check her mother's bridal portrait on one wall and a more recent photograph on the mantelpiece, totally ignoring all other photo-graphs, including those of herself.

It is my strong feeling that it was this period in Elizabeth's life, especially the cold, ill-timed and impersonal handling of her transi-tion to community living, which led to her depression and the "dual diagnosis" categorization. It is now accepted that Elizabeth under-stands almost everything that is said to her. Although she has been unable to speak, read or write since her childhood convulsions, she still manages to communicate by screaming or shrieking to protest unfamiliar activity. "Only the transmitter is broken" is one doctor's assessment.

At Elizabeth's new home, she lived with 3 other former institu-tional residents. One had schizophrenia but could speak and com-municate without difficulty. The other two were non-verbal like Elizabeth; one was also blind. None of her new companions had been in her former residence and it seemed to be an incompatible group. For example, the verbal resident was adept at baking cakes. When she created treats for her new housemates, and although they would enjoy them, they were unable to say "Thank you". Not understanding the lack of communication abilities of her room-mates, the baker would feel insulted and display her anger. Eventually, this was handled by moving the baker to a more appropriate setting where her talents could be verbally praised. The newly vacated room was given to Elizabeth's room-mate and Elizabeth was able to enjoy her beloved privacy. When another resident required long-term hospitalization and there remained only two residents with two attendants both night and day, Elizabeth was in her ultimate environment. Regardless, when the annual bereavement/separation season arrived, her disruptive behavior returned with the patterns of refusing food, screaming, becoming reclusive, and suffering both weight loss and constipation.

Eventually, another non-verbal lady moved in and Elizabeth became very distressed at having to share both her bedroom and her caregiver. She resented the loss of privacy she had enjoyed for a few months and would demonstrate her displeasure through several new demands such as insisting on being kissed goodnight last.

During this new transition, another major problem developed for Elizabeth – excessive menstrual discharge which led to a hysterectomy (ovaries left in). Unfortunately, when Haldol was prescribed for post-op agitation, Elizabeth developed neuroleptic malignant syndrome (NMS)—a fatal allergy to the drug. (If I had not been with her at one critical point to intervene and prevent her last dose of Haldol, I believe my daughter would have died.)

The unhappiness with the new roommate continued and, during one period in 1991, Elizabeth had major episodes of impatience, irritability, screaming, self-abuse and more weight loss. This finally was resolved and in winter of 1993, she had one of the best periods of her life. She thoroughly enjoyed the festive season and was content until early spring when once again the annual upset of her move from the hospital returned. Her disruptive behavior could not be controlled and it became obvious to everyone that she needed medical intervention.

This began the frantic search for appropriate mental health services that could treat these mal-adaptive behaviors.

With the concerted efforts of her superb "never-give-up" staff; her psychiatrist, her dedicated social worker and her family, Elizabeth was finally admitted in June to a hospital psychiatric ward in Vancouver. This was no small achievement because beds were usually not available for Developmentally Delayed people. What followed was a 70 day period of comprehensive treatment and follow-up by an exceptional psychiatric team who were relentless in getting to the causes of the problems.

After a medication adjustment between Anafranil and Paxil, Elizabeth's behavior improved greatly.

She even became quite content to sit calmly on her own in the lounge. The doctors' conclusion was that, in addition to her severe mental retardation, Elizabeth had fallen into a major depression. This depression kept recurring at times of anxiety such as the occasion of my heart surgery. The doctors were firm in their opinion that, to keep her on an even keel, Elizabeth's home life had to be kept structured and calm with every effort made to ensure her privacy.

Her social worker moved with the speed of light. Just a day and a half before discharge, the person sharing her room was moved and the 3-bedroom house permanently became a "3 resident" home. I brought in some new furnishings along with more family photos and paintings and the staff did an outstanding job in redecorating Elizabeth's room. They also arranged a special space for her in the common room. Soon Elizabeth returned to her former contentment. She enjoyed her private spaces and returned to sleeping peacefully.

Since then a dedicated, knowledgeable and sensitive home staff, assisted periodically by the mental health support team, have continued to provide exceptional supports and services. Staff members have been largely stable with the majority of them, including the manager, having a minimum of 15 years of continuous service. Amazingly, two of her personal one-to-one caregivers have been on staff since the day

Elizabeth moved in. Former staff members frequently return for friendly visits. The results of a recent accreditation survey give the management company "exemplary" ratings. These exceptional people have created a true family home for 3 unique residents.

In summary, the conclusion remains that Elizabeth was, and still is, suffering, inter alia, from a major depression. Very careful medical administration and fine-tuning adjustments with subsequent monitoring has resulted in a much more contented lady. (It should be noted that, by having Elizabeth in an extended hospital stay, the psychiatric unit was able to consult with other specialists who diagnosed and treated a number of formerly undetected physical problems. This included an ulcer at the pit of her stomach which clearly would have been causing some of her screaming episodes due to extreme pain. Being non-verbal, Elizabeth could not communicate her pain or any other unusual discomfort.)

Today, although she still has periodic upsets and continues to resist change, Elizabeth has a stable and comfortable life. All the staff members know her idiosyncrasies and are able to predict what she is going to do as well as react appropriately. They understand and honor her established rigid routines. She has a 1:1 staff member with her Monday to Friday as she still refuses to participate in any group day programs in the often noisy work room. It could be said that she began "early retirement" in 1994 after leaving the hospital psychiatric ward.

Each Saturday and Sunday I become her personal chauffeur for four hours. I believe that the car could drive itself because it has covered the same route for many years. ("It's MY way on the highway." "Yes, ma'am.") The route includes a brief visit to the nearly-demolished site of the old institution. Shortly after Elizabeth left the place, I had driven her back to see if she remembered it. Although she grinned in recollection when we entered the grounds, her smile turned to a frown when the car stopped in front of her old residence. Her hand moved to the car keys and she gave me a look that conveyed her immediate response and request. "Move it, man! I am NOT going in there again." I understood perfectly, and, with a "Yes, ma'am", we departed.

It took many more years to figure out and understand what other feelings Elizabeth had been communicating. Lately, when access to her records became available, I learned that although she had been allowed to walk around those beautiful heritage grounds by herself, she never wandered away. Her reaction to the visits to the site made things very clear. Although Elizabeth had actually disliked her former residence all those years, she loved the freedom and space of the grounds. Her solitary walks were the only times she was ever alone.

Most of the time these days, Elizabeth is the picture of contentment, a healthy woman with beautiful warm smiles. By the end of our weekend drives, her humming gets louder and louder, peaking when we enter her home driveway. By the time we reach the door, however, the message she conveys in her farewell look is very clear: "Ok, buster. You've done your job. I'm home. Now get lost." Again, my response is "Yes, ma'am" and, ever the dutiful servant, I leave her for another week.

Finally, after years of change and adjustment, challenges and survival, Elizabeth enjoys a relatively calm life. She still suffers through the annual emotional upheavals and she will always have anxieties and fears. She still needs a team of specialists and caregivers to provide her with the care she requires for stability and survival, but over all, her life is good. The safe home and secure surroundings she enjoys now were the original goals that her mother and I worked towards all her life. I feel so very satisfied to see that this special daughter has become a genuinely happy woman.

PERSONAL FOOTNOTE AND OBSERVATION:

Despite protests, the hospital's psychiatric ward was closed shortly after Elizabeth's discharge. This closure left only 25 beds for DD people at another clinic. In January 2005, this second facility was also phased out and replaced with a 10-bed unit with a 90 day maximum stay policy.

Question: Where do people like Elizabeth go if they need more than 90 days? It is a widespread belief that the current system does not seem to be equipped to handle these needs.

GARRY

Garry is now almost forty.

He demonstrated features of autism and intellectual disability from a young age. In adult life he developed epilepsy and problem behaviors. These issues were successfully treated with anticonvulsants and high doses of an antipsychotic medication called haloperidol. As his mother was concerned about long term side effects of high dose haloperidol, it was agreed to attempt to discontinue this medication under constant monitoring. During signs of instability of mood and/or the presence of environmental stress, the taper is temporarily stopped and then restarted. Over a period of 5 years, the haloperidol dose has been gradually reduced by approximately 60%.

—RF

GARRY'S STORY

His name is Garry and he is my beloved son, my only child. He was a beautiful baby and, by all appearances, perfectly normal and healthy. By the time he was four to six months old, it became apparent there was something amiss, although I could not identify just what it was.

We began a series of visits to different doctors, and eventually, when Garry was three years old, we were referred to a pediatrician at a large children's health centre. On three consecutive days Garry went through various tests, diagnostic procedures and examinations. Finally, we heard the word AUTISM, a word that had no previous meaning for us. The nightmare and heartache began to unfold slowly and painfully. As I learned more and more about Autism and the life-long consequences, I was devastated beyond belief. This devastation remained in my heart for many, many years.

Garry had no speech and repetitive obsessive behaviors occupied his private silent world. Although putting a handicapped child in the care of others may be an option for some, I could not, and I would not, leave my precious child under the care of anyone else. I felt that no one would know how to anticipate his needs as well as I could. My own life had to be put on hold as my plans and future goals were not compatible with my son's needs 24/7. My son became and remains my life.

Garry had to be toilet trained but the usual methods wouldn't work. There were no published methods on training an autistic child so, out of desperation, I developed my own. One day I locked myself in the bathroom with Garry, removed his diaper and the two of us spent six wrenching, exhausting hours without food or drink, just waiting and testing each other's patience. Finally Garry sat on the toilet and we had success. From that day on, he used the toilet.

Around this time, I met with the executive director of a newly opened facility where treatment for autistic children (behavior modification including force-feeding) was being introduced under the direction of a specialist from the u.s. Garry remained at the facility for some time and this was the first of many programs we used to help him. These were all very good people trying to help Garry the best they knew how at the time.

From age 6 on, if it was not raining, this very active, lovely little boy began to escape from the safety of home to explore the city on his own. It was truly terrifying to know in my heart how vulnerable he was and how easily anyone could just grab Garry off the street. This was an almost daily occurrence, but thankfully the city police kept an "open file" on him. They would need to search for him time and time again. Sometimes they would find him and other times, thanks to an identification bracelet with our phone number engraved, kind strangers would get him back home.

After the first program, Garry went to a special class at an elementary school where he had wonderful teachers. By this time, he could verbalize responses if the questions were formulated for a "Yes" or "No" answer and his eating issues had improved a bit. From there, he moved to another elementary school and was given a learning assistant who was responsible solely for Garry's needs. This was the very first school board-funded personal attendant, and was the beginning of mainstreaming in Vancouver.

As if all these changes weren't enough to challenge Garry, I decided that he needed to learn to use the public transit buses. We started with him using a bus to his community centre program once a week. For a whole month, I drove behind the bus to make sure he would get off at the right stop and then transfer to the next bus. Not only did he learn that route, but, to this day, Garry has an excellent knowledge of how the bus system works throughout the entire city. We learned that fact many years later when, without permission, he went on his own to the huge Pacific National Exhibition. He managed to get there in spite of having to transfer through three different bus routes! Even though Garry still does not appreciate the value of money, he does know the value of his bus pass and considers it to be a precious possession.

Over the years, I do remember how frustrating it was when Garry would not "fit" into programs where his peers were learning hobbies, sports or social skills. We tried all sorts of clubs and groups, even a scouting association and a swim club, but none of them proved to be suitable. We were lucky to have kind and gracious neighbors who owned a pool. They gave us a key to their yard and I was able to teach Garry to swim. This was a true gift from heaven as he could truly enjoy hot summer days.

When Garry reached his teens and moved to a special class at a high school, he had to learn a new bus route which, at times, involved two or more buses. I became not only Garry's advocate but also an advocate for all people with special needs. I contacted the public transit authority and urged them to educate their drivers on appropriate attitude, kinder treatment and better awareness of the needs of their developmentally disabled customers. My overtures to them may have seemed unusual but I knew change had to start somewhere and I was a determined mother.

Garry left his first high school because we felt there was very little tolerance and understanding from regular students and even from some teachers. He transferred to a school for the mentally handicapped for a short time and then to a work-related program. The work program was a good one but had a very large number of participants. Due to Garry's autism, the number of students along with the accompanying noise level made the experience overwhelming and intolerable. He left the program and we were out of options.

Garry's father never did accept his son's disability. As time passed, I was doing more and more on my own and finding it increasingly more difficult to cope. To say that our marriage was falling apart would be the understatement of the millennium. I was wearing down fast and hardly able to function. The tense and unhappy environment was hard on Garry, too, and finally, social workers and other professionals recommended that he be placed in a foster home. I knew that Garry needed relief from the hell that home had become, but still, after years of keeping him safe, I felt very guilt-ridden to relinquish the care of my beloved son to a complete stranger.

As it turned out, the "complete stranger" was the best thing to ever happen to both of us. Garry became much more independent, more helpful with doing chores, more responsible and more receptive to sharing with others. And I came aware of the reality that I needed to let go more. In my obsessive need to protect and shelter, I had been wearing myself out. I had been doing everything for Garry and nothing for myself. I had given myself sleepless nights, suicidal thoughts and self-loathing in my misguided attempts to prove my undying love for my child, to perhaps prove I could love him enough for both parents. This, in the end, was unhealthy for both of us.

It is a well documented fact that many marriages do not survive the devastation of having a child born with a lifelong developmental disability. This is especially true if one of the parents can not accept the diagnosis. Even though Garry's father and I went to counseling, I could never get over the fact that his father was jealous and resentful of the attention I gave to our only son. There were other personal issues as well, insurmountable ones, and our marriage couldn't be salvaged. It was important for my own sanity that I completely remove myself from the old situation and so, without a job or much of anything else, I left.

Garry did not accept the divorce very well at all. He had adapted to his move to the foster home but he couldn't comprehend the realities of the divorce and his former home being split up. It broke my heart to see his reaction and I spent a lot of time trying to soothe his anxiety.

Initially I could only find part-time jobs but then got a fulltime position and often worked seven days a week to build a new life for us. I was determined to succeed on my own and I did. Eventually I was able to develop a routine where I could pick Garry up on my day off and we could spend quality time together. While I had been getting established, Garry had been spending weekends with his father. Although I had been hoping that this was time spent in getting them to be closer, I discovered that his father was leaving him unsupervised for hours at a time late into the night. With the risks of this arrangement being obvious, the social workers ended the weekend stays away from the group home.

To his credit, Garry's father began to visit him there, but the reaction from Garry was almost predictable. He was just not interested. The minute his father showed up at the door, he would take off in the opposite direction. Then, one day, Garry decided he no longer wished to see his father at all. He also decided—on his own—that he wished to be known only by his second name, Garry. He had been baptized as Matthew Garry and had always been known by Matthew, his father's name, but now he made a point of telling everyone that he was now officially to be called Garry. To this day he responds only to the name he has chosen.

I am a practicing Roman Catholic and my belief requires that I raise my child in the Catholic faith. When Garry was about fourteen years old, I enquired about religious education for him. To my amazement, the Catholic Church in the Vancouver diocese did not have any programs in place for those with developmental disabilities. Once again Garry did not fit the system and once again I embarked on a quest to remedy a shameful situation. My goal was to convince the people in charge that religious education is not only a right of everyone—including the handicapped—but it is also guaranteed by the teachings of the Catholic Church. They have a moral obligation to provide it. It took many sleepless nights to formulate my approach and many strong words to communicate the aggressive steps I intended to take. My efforts were finally instrumental in establishing a new education program for developmentally challenged parishioners. Garry attended every Saturday morning for three years and, eventually, he received the sacraments to become a full member of the Catholic Church. The Archbishop of Vancouver and I even became good friends again. (Today, the five programs throughout Vancouver and the Lower Mainland function at full capacity and in 2006, the Sisters of Saint Mary of Providence will celebrate twenty-five years in Vancouver, teaching developmentally disabled children religious education.)

We knew that many autistic males develop epilepsy by age 25 and sure enough, three weeks before his 25th birthday, Garry had the first of nineteen grand mal seizures. My beloved son suffered terribly and, as luck would have it, he had all of the seizures away from home. Sometimes, in the middle of the street, he would collapse to the ground. Each time he would end up in hospital. Many times he was badly hurt. He had broken teeth, a broken wrist, cuts on his face and gashes in his head requiring stitches. As he refused to carry identification, I sewed his name on all his clothing. This gave me peace of mind knowing that the ambulance attendants and hospital would have someone to call.

Garry has been gradually maturing and his vocabulary has expanded. He still uses the repetitive phrases that are a trait of autism. He always has been very good-natured and peaceful and sometimes this has placed him in dangerous situations. Thankfully, he eventually learned to defend himself when cornered or pushed to his limit.

In 1996, Garry was very fortunate to be referred to the West Coast Mental Health Support Team, and become a patient of Dr. Robin Friedlander. I believe this was heaven sent. Garry is doing so very well, and I personally feel this is due not only to the doctor's knowledge and experience but also in his genuine interest in my son's wellbeing and the closer monitoring of his medication and behaviors. Numerous drugs had failed to control Garry's seizures for almost seven years but today, his medications seem to working for him and he has been seizure-free for six years.

Yes, there were years that I questioned: WHY ME? I have since come to realize the obvious: Why NOT me?

I am better equipped to care for, to accept and to love my son than anyone else. I have the added help of my faith which has been a very important element in maintaining my strength and daily fortitude. I feel very blessed to have discovered that unconditional love is the purest, most exquisite, most profound feeling in the world. I would not change this kind of love for anything. I would do it all over again in a heartbeat. Every day, I give thanks for having Garry as my beloved son. My devotion to him remains constant and there are times when my heart physically aches to see him go through difficult times. My only wish for the future is that he remains safe, sound and happy.

TRACY

Tracy is a patient of one of my colleagues.

One of our own nurses knew that Tracy expressed herself through poetry and she felt that Tracy could provide another aspect to this book. Was she ever right!

—RF

TRACY'S STORY

Tracy is my real name. I didn't want to write a story about my life, but I did want to contribute something to this book that might explain how I feel. I wrote my own thoughts in the form of a poem. I hope my words will help other people think.

"A LITTLE ABOUT ME"
I may shake from time to time in my hands,
I am a very good hand shaker, when I come to meet people.
I may sound funny to others
I have a beautiful voice for poetry.
I may be a slower learner in some areas of my life
I am a fast thinker when it comes down to people I care about.
I may not look perfect on the outside
I am full of love and kindness on the inside.
I may be shy to strangers
I am a chatter box when I come to know them.
I have a lot of sad days in my life
I have a humor that keeps me going each day.
I can be frustrated at times in my life
I am very patient with others.
I do not cry too much on the outside
I cry a lot on the inside.
I want a happy future
I am working on getting my happy future.

—*Tracy*

SEAN

Sean is in his mid-twenties.

He was 12 years old when a pediatrician asked me to see him about anger outbursts.

Sean was known to have an intellectual disability, but associated autism had not yet been diagnosed. His frustration was exacerbated by both the constant teasing from his brother and the difficulty he had in expressing himself due to articulation difficulties.

In late adolescence, Sean began hearing voices and manifested extreme irritability. Although his moods and hallucinations are handled much better when he is on medication, Sean resents taking them. After huge power struggles with his caregivers became a serious issue, our nurse negotiated a deal with Sean. We keep his medications at the lowest level possible and he takes them on a regular basis as prescribed. So far the deal is working!

—RF

SEAN'S STORY

After an uneventful pregnancy, Sean's delivery into the world was difficult. Although my water had been seeping, the contractions weren't forthcoming and the labor had to be induced. Finally, with the assistance of forceps, my healthy 8 lb., 11 oz. son was born. He was breastfed for 13 weeks and then, two weeks later, I returned to my office duties at a community school.

As a first-time, inexperienced mother, I was unique in my group of friends. Thankfully, I not only worked with pregnant mothers but also with children in the toddler stage right up to grade sevens. Health nurses came for regular visits and I was able to participate in the group sessions with pre and postnatal mothers. I could address any concerns I had about my own child. Sean cried a lot but he was not colicky. He sat up, crawled, walked and fed himself at the right stages.

When Sean's speech seemed to be different from other babies and he was still not talking well by the age of two, the nurses suggested that I get involved with the infant development program at the health clinic. As part of the program, Sean attended a special needs preschool/daycare that was integrated with typical children. During this time, he went twice to the hospital for testing. The diagnosis was that Sean had a mild intellectual disability, a speech disorder and behavioral problems (OCD and anger tantrums). We were told that he would reach his maximum learning potential by the age of sixteen.

Of all his problems, Sean's behavior became the most troublesome and the whole family suffered, especially his younger brother.

We did receive support from the Provincial Ministry of Children and Families but, in our years spent consulting with specialists in many different fields, we never seemed to make any progress. When Sean was 14, we were referred to Dr. Robin Friedlander, who diagnosed him as having Asperger's Syndrome. Finally, we had a name for the illness that had overtaken our son and he began to take Prozac to help control his behavioral problems. Having a "label" was the best thing that could have happened to Sean as now we were able to get the help needed from the government and the school board.

Sean's brother continued to resent all the attention that we had to give Sean and all the time that we directed to handling his problem behavior. Instead of avoiding situations with Sean, he did his best to upset him. It became impossible to leave the two of them alone. The Ministry eventually suggested that it would be in the family's best interests, Sean's in particular, if we put him into foster care. A wonderful foster home was found when Sean was almost 16. He lived there during the week and came home every weekend. It was a relief to share the burden of Sean's behavior with someone else. The foster family was very supportive and we were able to function better emotionally by having the weekdays to heal.

Over the next three years, and during his difficult times with secondary school, Sean was moved three times. But he finally graduated and when he turned 19, he moved into a group home and found two small part-time jobs.

The plan was for Sean to continue to spend weekends at home but, as the weekends were still very stressful, we changed the arrangement so that Sean would spend only 3 weekends a month with us. He did not accept this change very well and continues to punish himself and everyone else for this change in his routine. On the weekends that he must remain at the group home, he is non-communicative. On the weekends when he does come home, he punishes me for not allowing him to be home more.

Even though he does not have the ability to read or write, Sean has a very intelligent mind. He can sight read, memorize words, copy phrases, and sign his name. He can remember travel routes as well. He is a very angry person most of the time but can be very polite and pleasant if required. This validates my belief that he can control his behavior at will.

Sean starts to hear voices if he doesn't take his medicine (Olanzapine) and then he feels that certain things are out to "get him" (paranoia). He gets frustrated and fed up at having to take any of the medicines; he feels he doesn't need it. Although he is cooperating for now, we feel that it is only a matter of time before he will stop. Now that he is an adult and knows that he has rights, he also knows that we can not force him to take medication. He has been to the psychiatric ward at the hospital more than once, being apprehended and admitted by the police a few times. When things have upset him a lot, he has even tried to commit himself.

Since having Sean, we have learned what it means to live day by day. We remain positive and even dream that one day our son will become a happy and compliant adult, an adult whose company we could enjoy. We are so very grateful that at least we live in a country where families and patients have continued assistance from government agencies and where there are support groups to help us all cope with the unique difficulties associated with developmental disabilities and mental disorders.

RIIA

When we were planning this book, a suggestion was made that we might be able to find a talented patient to do the artwork for the cover. We spread the word through all the clinics in the district and Riia was nominated by one of my colleagues. After meeting her and viewing her work, we were convinced that she was the right person for the job.

Riia has Obsessive Compulsive Disorder (OCD) and is a very talented artist. Her images speak volumes.

—RF

RIIA'S STORY

Riia is my real name.

I am twenty years old and I have Obsessive Compulsive Disorder. Looking back I realize this problem has been with me all my life, although it was not diagnosed until I was fifteen years old. At that point I began to understand that the time consuming routines I did, the lists I made and the repetitious thoughts I had were largely a result of this disorder. Up until this time I had thought "this is just who I am and this is just the way I do things".

I have always had a love for art and, as far back as I can remember, I have used drawing and painting as a way to let out my emotions. As soon as I picked up a pencil or brush, I began creating. When I was drawing or painting, I was in my own world: a world of people, animals, shapes or color.

Strangely enough, being finally diagnosed with OCD was a blessing in many ways. I learned that one in every fifty adults has this disorder and that I am not alone. Checking repeatedly to see if the door is locked, writing out list after list of things I need to do and becoming anxious or even fearful of everyday happenings are things that others do as well.

As I learned more about this disorder I began a series of paintings about OCD. My art has been shown in a number of community galleries and I was interviewed on the Delta Cable TV show "Arts Around Town". My work was displayed in a three-person group show at Gallery Cachet in Vancouver where I received a favorable review in "Only" Magazine.

There are good days and there are bad days but I find that as I learn to gain control of my situation, the good days are starting to win out.

I didn't write a long story about my life for this book. Instead, I provided eight of my paintings that illustrate my feelings and progress. One of my paintings was also selected to be photographed for the cover of this book and I am very proud of my accomplishments.

"GO AWAY"

Medium: Chalk pastel on canvas, 16" x 20"

This is a young woman using her own hand to shield herself from the hands of OCD

GREEN DANCER

Medium: Chalk pastel on canvas, 16" x 20"

The green dancing figure in the background is trying to draw
the happiness and joy from the spotlighted purple dancer

"NIGHT OBSESSION"

Medium: Chalk pastel and water on canvas, 16" x 20"

This painting represents an ocd victim who is distraught because she is obsessing about checking and rechecking the doorknob to ensure it is locked. She knows it is locked but she continues to obsess and worry.

"OCD STRESS"

Medium: Acrylic on canvas, 16" x 20"

The figure on the left is trying to summon the determination required to face the challenges of the day. The figure on the right has withdrawn and tries to cloak himself for protection.

"OCD SPREADS ALL OVER ME"

Medium: Chalk pastel on canvas, 9" x 12"

The painting represents the body of a victim being slowly overtaken by the OCD. The dots represent the OCD spreading. It can start by creeping into your brain—very slowly at first and then faster and faster until the thoughts get stuck inside and soon your whole body is consumed by the OCD.

"STOPPING THE LIME COLORED HAND"

Medium: Chalk pastel on canvas, 16" x 20"

The lime-colored hand represents an OCD victim who is reaching up to turn off the light switch. The purple represents the need to keep it on. Simple everyday decisions can become the cause of internal conflict for many people with OCD.

"THE THREE MASKS OF OCD"

Medium: Acrylic and oil pastel on canvas, 16" x 20"

The central figure is in the light because he is free from OCD for the moment. The figure behind him is the OCD waiting to take over once again. On the right, the man in the shadows is trying to protect himself with a cloak of red

"GOOD DAYS"

Medium: Acrylic on canvas, 12″ x 16″

The figure and objects represent me and my feelings
when the OCD is not in control.

JASMINE

Jasmine is now in her twenties. She was born in Vietnam and arrived in Canada with her family as a refugee.

From an early age her parents were aware of the intellectual disability associated with Jasmine's autism and epilepsy.

Severe hyperactivity requires constant supervision and Jasmine's behavior has always been a real handful for her family. At one stage we wondered if some of her irritability was due to a mood disorder, but this initial diagnosis proved to be without merit.

We have the most incredible respect for her mother's dedication to looking after her adult daughter. Jasmine weighs twice as much as this gentle woman. She is also much taller than her mom and she can mightily tug her away when she decides she is ready to leave the office.

—RF

JASMINE'S STORY

My daughter Jasmine was born in Vietnam in 1978. She suffered her first epileptic seizure when she was seven months old. At that time, South Vietnam had fallen into communist hands and medical services were not very good. Although my daughter stayed at the local hospital for a month, the staff was unable to stop the seizures and they simply sent her home. The seizures continued to occur once or twice a month and we had no explanation of the cause.

In 1979, our family escaped by boat to Indonesia. The first day at sea, Jasmine had a seizure and the seizures continued frequently throughout both the journey and during our seven months' stay in a refugee camp in Indonesia. There was little we could do to help her. We had no money to buy food so certainly there was nothing for medical attention or medications.

Fortunately, the Canadian Government accepted us as refugees and we settled in northern BC. Jasmine's seizures continued and often the intensity of them forced us to rush her to the hospital. Finally in 1981, the doctors in our small town sent her to Vancouver for an assessment at the large children's hospital. Since I could not speak English, the government agencies would not approve the cost for me to accompany Jasmine. We spent the entire month without any updates or information about our little girl. Even after she was returned home, we never were given any reports or results.

Another year passed with no improvement and then the doctors sent Jasmine back to Vancouver, this time to a different hospital. By this time, I could speak a little English and after much insistence, they allowed me to accompany her. Everyone at the hospital was very kind, but Jasmine had become a very hyperactive four-year old and I was exhausted between trying to keep up with her and attending all the conferences with the professionals. After a week, I had to leave her there to return to my employment and take care of my family back home.

In spite of the new assessments, consultations, and medications, Jasmine's seizures were continuing at the same rate. As all the specialists were in Vancouver, I convinced my husband to move there so that we could get specialized medical attention for our daughter. It was still another four years before we were given an official diagnosis—Jasmine had both epilepsy and autism.

Jasmine attended a school for the mentally handicapped for three years and then attended a regular secondary school for six years. When she was nineteen years old, as she entered her final year in the school system, we were told that Jasmine would soon have to spend all her days at home as there was no funding available from the government agencies for other programs for her.

As I must work full time to support the family, staying at home was not an option for me. I began to insist on getting the support we needed. Jasmine's social worker managed to persuade the School Board to extend the school program for one more year and Jasmine transferred to another school. By the end of the year, we received approval for funding in an adult day program.

During all this time, it was very hard on our family to provide full time care for Jasmine. She can not communicate and doesn't seem to understand what we say to her. She needs help with all her personal care; her autism is profound, she is extremely hyper-active and her actions are often dangerous and self-abusive. She requires constant supervision as she does not understand even basic personal safety. In addition, perhaps due to her autism, she has great difficulty in adjusting to any changes in her schedule or environment.

Once Jasmine became older and became more aware of her limitations, her distress with this knowledge became very evident.

Nothing we did seemed to cheer her up and her self-abuse worsened. Fortunately she was referred to an excellent mental health team and they all became very involved in helping both Jasmine and the family.

I am very thankful to be living in Canada where I can get good medical attention for Jasmine. Her psychiatrist and the entire mental health team have been very supportive throughout these trying times and their commitment has been unwavering. Our family has also had some dedicated and caring social workers who have worked very hard to get appropriate help for Jasmine and our family.

The stress has taken its toll on all aspects of our lives including my marriage. For the past two years, I have had the sole responsibility for Jasmine as I am now a single working mother. Due to my shift work hours/days not matching the schedule of the day program, I not only must use our respite allowance to cover the overlap days but must also pay the extra $21.90 usage fee per day. Once we have exhausted the allocated respite days just to enable me to work fulltime, I must pay the full cost of each day myself. These added expenses have a serious impact on our already-stretched budget. With the respite funding required for daily survival, there are no days of rest or respite available and I am burning out very quickly.

In October 2005, my work schedule was changed to 10:00 am till 6:00 pm. Since the day program ends at 3:00 pm, I needed a support worker to care for Jasmine between 3:00-6:30 pm Although I pleaded for help, none came and we endured more than six months of even more stress. Jasmine would be sitting in tears each day when I got home and this broke my heart. Recently I was able to change my shift to 6 am to 3 pm. Jasmine's father is currently coming to our home very early in the morning to care for her until 9 am and I am there when she returns from her program in the afternoon. Unfortunately, this is a temporary arrangement.

Thankfully, Jasmine's older brother does not live too far. He loves his sister dearly and is able to help out occasionally. Her younger brother is not as mature and, through no fault of his own, he simply can not deal with Jasmine's many needs. I do have to rely on his minimal supervision at times but this is not a good situation for Jasmine.

At present, Jasmine's seizures are controlled with medications but the struggle continues. Although the day program works for many families, it is not ideal for us as it is relatively inflexible. We are currently seeking an alternative way to support Jasmine—a way that will allow her to feel secure, to remain at home and a way to give the family a less stressful future.

I find it very frustrating to know that if Jasmine were placed in a group home or in foster care, the provincial government would easily spend in excess of $200,000 a year for her care, including transportation, housing, staffing and living costs. Even so, a group home placement is just not an option. Jasmine would not be happy separated from me and I would agonize daily over her wellbeing. Ironically, a financial commitment of one-third of that amount made directly to the family could provide consistent supervision, a planned activity program and transportation. It could also ensure that Jasmine would be able to remain in her secure and loving home environment indefinitely.

Things are changing in the way some services for the disabled are going to be managed. We are now learning about some programs being developed and are working towards making some positive changes to Jasmine's support and funding. Hopefully the next year will see a better life for all of us.

MARTIN

Martin is in his early forties. Sometimes I see him walking by the beach with his support worker. As Martin isn't expecting to see me out of the office setting, he just carries on walking, eyes straight ahead, with no obvious recognition.

Martin had a childhood diagnosis of ID and autism. Behavioral problems began when he was an adult and he was treated at the University Hospital with a medication called Luvox (Fluvoxamine) to target symptoms of OCD. This medication helped control the OCD, but then Martin became excessively driven (drug induced mania) and he was referred to me about ten years ago.

Treatment with an antipsychotic medication successfully treated the mania, but, unfortunately, he developed side effects from it (Tardive Dyskineisa). Attempts to stop all his medication were not possible as his behavior problems were too severe. Currently, the best results are achieved with a low dose of one of the original antipsychotic medications.

Martin's parents are pretty amazing people. They have "gone the extra mile" by keeping their son busy and by adapting their lives to his in order to cope with his OCD.

—RF

MARTIN'S STORY

Martin has always lived at home with us.

Shortly after his birth, he was diagnosed as having Minimum Brain Dysfunction. With the added problems of multiple food allergies, asthma and Celiac disease, his life has been a constant challenge. Nonetheless, we all managed to cope with the situation and Martin developed from a fairly happy boy into a contented young man.

Ten years ago, when his grandfather died, everything took a turn for the worse. Martin became depressed and manic, his moods swinging swiftly from high to low and his manner becoming very aggressive towards everyone. Almost overnight he changed into a hyperactive, obsessive-compulsive dynamo with unpredictable behavior.

With the addition of this mental illness, Martin now required anti-psychotic drugs and we embarked on a journey of trial and error, using one new drug after another trying to stabilize his condition. Many of the drugs caused disastrous results such as worsened behavior and heightened displays of his Obsessive Compulsive Disorder. Some things we regularly deal with are:

Sometimes Martin can't stop eating and drinking. We keep most food locked up on a separate floor.

Martin only eats with certain spoons and forks and if we can't find them, he won't eat until we do.

We use Kleenex in the bathroom because he can't refrain from unrolling an entire roll of toilet tissue and putting it down the toilet.

Anything in the house that is bottled, whether it is gin or salad dressing or liquid cleanser; anything that we forget to lock up, Martin fills to the top with water.

Everything Martin owns must be in threes and everything he

does must be done in threes: three combs/ three hair combings, three tooth brushes/ three brushings—all tasks must be done three times before he can go for a walk.

Inside our home we can easily cope with all his needs but outside the house it's another story. Martin is obsessed with garbage: papers, pop cans, wine bottles, anything. If our doors were not kept locked, he would always be down the back lanes picking up everyone's garbage and recyclables and bringing them home.

When he was taking one drug, Martin would remove all the garbage from one neighbor's trashcans and then pile it all up in another neighbor's cans. When he was finished his cleanup project, he would come home exhausted but very happy after doing such a great job! I would then begin *my* job replacing the garbage, hopefully in the right containers.

On another anti-psychotic drug, every day for five months, he took all the neighborhood garbage cans and lined them up at the end of the lane. They would be lined up in exactly the same order every day.

This job would take one to two hours to complete, depending on the weight of the cans, and each time Martin would contentedly come home and fall asleep. Once he was asleep, I went back on his route and replaced everything so the cans would be ready for the next day's work.

We continue to play "do the lane" once a week. A half hour before Martin is ready to go out, I sneak down the lane and deposit my own supply of wine bottles, pop bottles, soap containers, plant pots, gardening trays, newspapers and firewood by each neighbor's fence. Then Martin and I go out together on his "rounds" and he brings everything home. As Martin can recognize labels and packaging, I try to keep a wide selection of recycled containers and bottles on hand. The neighbors know what is going on and they are very understanding.

A caregiver has joined our unusual work crew and so now we have assistance with "doing the lane". After Martin does the first house, we distract him enough to get him back in the car. He is not as agile anymore, so the caregiver and I can hop out quickly and retrieve all the other things. When his lane job is done and he's back home, Martin goes through all his other rituals, including piling the fire-wood in exact rows, filling some bottles with water and lining up the others. Once his jobs are done, he's ready to go out in the car or go for a hike or a walk.

We have learned to divert and distract Martin, sometimes with success, sometimes not. We try to avoid walking by display racks of brochures but they seem to be everywhere. Sometimes Martin can be persuaded to take just a few things but usually he takes the whole lot. He hoards papers, plastic bags, pamphlets and business cards. We would not be able to move in our home if we didn't take some the materials away but we can only sneak things out if he doesn't see us. If he caught us removing his "collections", he would get very upset and even aggressive. I feel that sometimes he's relieved to have some things removed but he never says so in words and I'm always pre-pared to bring things back if there is a problem.

At the moment Martin is thinking more clearly and his behavior is improved. Although his Tardive Dyskinesia is very bad he doesn't seem bothered by it. We live in hope that life will improve for all of us down the road.

MELODY

Melody is almost 21. Her parents recognized her developmental delays in childhood and have adapted their lives accordingly.

At the age of 12, Melody first presented with psychotic symptoms (hallucinations and delusions). At first these symptoms seemed like fantasy, but, over time, it became clear that she was developing a schizophrenic illness. (It should be noted that one of my colleagues disagreed with the diagnosis of schizophrenia).

Once the psychosis was treated, Melody had her first epileptic seizure. There most likely had always been an underlying vulnerability to epilepsy and we would now categorize her as belonging to the specific subgroup of young people who have epilepsy and who have an increased risk of developing psychotic disorders such as schizophrenia.

Her parents continue to be her strongest advocates.

—RF

MELODY'S STORY

Our daughter Melody was born in 1986, in France. Other than the foreign location, nothing about the pregnancy or the birth indicated she would grow to be extraordinary in every sense of the word. Although her childhood seemed normal, in the clearer vision of "hindsight", we acknowledge that there actually were some early hints of future difficulties.

Our daughter had frequent temper tantrums but these were accepted merely as unpleasant moments. We just let the storms run their course. Rational argument fell on deaf ears so we handled them with powerless distance. Later we realized that these tantrums were actually subtle indications of latent psychotic episodes.

Melody's introverted nature and her preference to play alone was considered to be an indication of shyness—an acceptable, if not admired, personality trait. We certainly did not view this as an inability to socialize normally. We even considered her talking to imaginary friends to be within the bounds of normality. Oddly repetitive habits were curious but certainly not viewed as compulsive behavior.

We also underestimated any problem with Melody's speech. Although she began to talk later than most average children, she eventually spoke in two languages!

It was not until Melody began kindergarten that we began to have any real concerns. She seemed to respond in an unusual manner to many commands and she had difficulty in acquiring physical dexterity. (She never did learn to ride a bicycle or catch a ball.) She preferred to be by herself and any child who isolates herself from a classroom of five year olds quickly draws attention.

The irony of my own delay in picking up on all the combined

signals is that I happen to be a primary teacher. Perhaps because my training allowed me to reason that all children learn at different rates, I concluded that Melody just needed time to develop at her own pace. Sadly, the ability of a parent to deny a stark unwanted truth about her own child can never be underestimated!

The gap between what I wanted to believe and what was actually the truth became evident two years later when I received the results of Melody's first Psychological Educational test. Intellectually, I could accept that an I.Q. of 55 is devastating for any child's future. Emotionally, I felt it difficult to comprehend or believe the extent of this revelation for my own daughter. But time is a teacher as well as a healer.

By Grade Two, with Melody now being officially diagnosed as being "mildly mentally handicapped", we became her advocates and made certain that she had a full time Special Education Assistant to aid her in the classroom.

Outside of periodic tantrums during these elementary school years, Melody was a sweet, generous, and lovely child. She learned very slowly but life continued as our family divided our time between Canada and France. The naïve calm that we enjoyed, however, was short-lived.

As the daughter of a mentally ill, alcoholic parent, I was painfully familiar with some of the symptoms of mental illness. When Melody began expressing alarming ideas at age 12, I knew that we had to be very watchful. When I talked to her about some new habits she was exhibiting, she lamented that "things inside of me" were making her do it. She begged us to take her to a doctor who could "cut them out of me". Subsequently, the ambiguous 'them' inside of her became "little black men that were building machines in my tummy". As well, an entire 'anti' family of evil members materialized. When I told our family physician of my growing concerns, he immediately referred us to a psychiatrist who specialized in the dual diagnosis of children with both mental retardation and mental illness.

Melody could distinguish between imaginary and real things inside of her, but she responded to the imaginary as if it was real. Melody's complaints were very intense but, as they were still relatively infrequent, her doctor suggested we closely monitor the situation rather than medicate immediately.

Two years passed, one of them in France. Upon our return, Melody became increasingly agitated and complained more frequently of the 'little black men' who were torturing her, controlling her behavior and causing her to be 'bad.' "Bad" included writing on herself, carving on the furniture, writing on the walls, cutting her clothes, destroying photos she previously loved, and wetting her bed. A small dose of Risperdal was prescribed but, by the summer of her sixteenth birthday, the mental illness that had been slowly progressing declared itself in a dramatic and terrifying manner.

New symptoms suddenly were added: having an aversion to the color red [food, clothes, paintings, everything red], cutting her hair, throwing furniture, hitting us, running down the driveway scantily clothed, repeatedly threatening to kill herself by jumping out of her second floor bedroom window, verbally abusing us, and finally, attempting to hold my head under the water at the local swimming pool. (As Melody weighs 200 lbs compared to my own svelte 130, it was an unfair contest). We contacted her psychiatrist and Melody was committed as an emergency to the adolescent psychiatry ward. Following a week of observation she was diagnosed with schizophrenia. After a month she returned home. Then the 'fun' began as we attempted to discover which anti-psychotic drugs would be most effective with the least side-effects.

Risperdal was replaced with Zyprexa which was replaced with Seroquel. None worked very well. Side effects included weight gain, tremors, and drug induced fatigue. After a year, Melody's condition was worsening so her doctor suggested a trial of Clozapine. This necessitated blood tests which Melody feared and she refused to cooperate.

Melody continued to deteriorate so, in the summer of 2003, she was admitted to the local hospital's adolescent psychiatric unit. She still refused to take any blood tests necessary to make the changes in drugs. In spite of this defiance, though, the doctors were able to observe our daughter more closely and analyze her symptoms. The head psychiatrist at this hospital questioned the previous diagnosis of schizophrenia and stated her belief that Melody actually had a major anxiety disorder. She felt that this was the reason the anti-psychotic medications were relatively ineffective and she prescribed a program of Effexor and Zyprexa. Although this combination was considerably effective, it was still far from perfect.

In spite of the magic that modern chemicals can accomplish, they can also create their own complications. Epilepsy is just one example. In February 2004 Melody had two grand mal seizures and was rushed into emergency. The MRI revealed nothing abnormal but she was prescribed Tegretol. The seizures disappeared for six months but then resumed in the form of drop seizures. She would lose consciousness and fall suddenly, often leaving her with bloody knees and a bruised face. (She wears knee pads now.) When Tegretol was replaced with Topomax, disaster struck in the form of increased, uncontrolled seizures. When Topomax was replaced with Lamictal in April, 2004, a slow improvement in the form of decreased seizure activity began. Things have changed from daily drop seizures and absence seizures with occasional grand mal seizures to a routine of a grand mal or series of drop seizures every two weeks. Melody's neurologist, a specialist in Epilepsy, has confidence (hopes) that a refined increase in Lamictal may lead to more improvement.

Melody is mentally handicapped, has a significant mental illness about which psychiatrists have differing opinions, and she stoically endures the added imposition of epilepsy. Experimentation with various medications has led to a decrease in the frequency, intensity, duration, of the seizures and the aftereffects of the mental illness 'episodes'.

Sometimes, when people ask: 'How is your daughter doing these days?" I want to reply: "Compared to whom?"

In spite of her handicaps, our daughter finished high school working within a skills development program. She participates in a day program with a community-based society and she enjoys their activities immensely. She has friends. She is enthusiastic about music, drawing, swimming, eating, dancing, reading and looking at her many books. She enjoys watching her videos, hugging her stuffed animals, going to the movies, and playing in the park. Melody is doing very well in this comparative sense.

She has always received excellent medical attention and appropriate medication. She has three competent doctors to deal with different aspects of her health and she is monitored regularly to keep her on an even keel. She has always had personal and emotional support from a nurturing family. She is loved.

Melody lives at home with her family where she is safe and secure and where she continues to give us much to ponder. It is frightening to think of what may have become of her if she not had been born into our family or had not been born in these times.

NEELIA

Neelia is now in her mid-twenties. Always regarded as a gentle young woman, well beloved by her family and community, Neelia was first assessed in kindergarten and was noted to have a mild intellectual disability.

We first met Neelia and her family when she was in her early teens. She had been previously diagnosed with early onset schizophrenia complicated by significant loss of skills and had been referred to our team for follow-up.

Neelia's journey was long and difficult. She suffered from teasing at school and became depressed and angry. Her caring mother became the target of her frustration and the family struggled for years as they tried to care for Neelia.

Over twelve years have passed and life—for everyone—seems to be improving.

—RF

NEELIA'S STORY

By the time Neelia turned three, I was convinced that something was not quite "right" with my daughter. She had always been extremely quiet, almost withdrawn. We hoped it was just a sign of shyness and enrolled her in a day care program so that playmates and new experiences would help bring her out of her shell. Unfortunately nothing changed. It wasn't long before we noticed that she could not remember what she did a few hours earlier. Then she began to bite herself on the wrist (This habit still exists, although with less frequency.) and her entire demeanor began to change.

After we met with the family doctor, he referred Neelia to the hospital for evaluation. Due to her young age, the doctors felt that the test results were inconclusive, and asked that they be repeated at age 5. After Neelia began kindergarten, the tests were repeated and the conclusion was that our daughter had a mild learning disability. She functioned at approximately two years below her chronological age. With the recommendation of the doctors, we got Neelia a personal aide at her school and hoped for the best.

Neelia continued to progress in her own quiet, obedient way – always passive, never aggressive. Although she didn't make friends at school, a few neighborhood children who were her age became regular playmates. These were happy times for Neelia. She was in a comfortable environment and we were pleased to see her interact with peers. Her big brother nicknamed her "Sparky" and we enjoyed a fairly calm period.

That was at home. School was another matter. Teachers did not seem to know how to work with Neelia. They constantly complained that she did not focus or participate. By the age of eleven, things became even more difficult. Neelia was forgetting how to read simple words and she could no longer focus on even basic math. Her aide was regularly expressing frustration at working with her.

When Neelia arrived home after school she would lie on the floor in front of the TV and scribble in a workbook for hours. During those times she also began to wash her hands so frequently and so vigorously that the skin was peeling and blistering. This compulsive behavior continued for months.

Just after her twelfth birthday, Neelia entered puberty and began her menstrual cycle. By summer, she would sit on a chair in our living room for hours, neither looking left or right, in an almost catatonic state. Occasionally, she would start to giggle and, when I asked her what was so funny, she would respond with "I don't know".

When Neelia's second period arrived, I wasn't aware of it until bedtime. She had not recognized that anything was different with her body and so had not said a word about it to me. For the following months, I began monitoring her personal needs more closely and, once the periods arrived, it became my job to attend to the changing and cleansing as this was beyond Neelia's capability.

Understanding my concerns, our family physician referred Neelia to a pediatric psychiatrist, who in turn referred us to the local mental health unit. When I called to make an appointment I was told that it could be a six month wait.

Meanwhile, in addition to an increase in the spontaneous giggling, Neelia began hearing voices. Initially I felt that she may have actually been talking to herself. (At that time, I was not familiar with the fact that some mental illnesses cause people to hear outside voices). When the voices continued to increase, I called the mental health office again. There was still a waiting period of at least six months. As my concern for my daughter was growing daily, I started calling the office incessantly. I stressed the fact that Neelia was not only a mentally handicapped twelve year old with limited understanding but that she was hearing voices and becoming totally confused. When they asked if she was trying to kill herself, I said "no, but if she doesn't get help immediately, things could easily escalate to that point." We got an appointment.

In the early sessions, Neelia could not explain her feelings, but could talk about the voices she was hearing. Sometimes the voices swore at her; sometimes there was one man's voice; sometimes there were lots of voices. She did not know what the voices were saying. After 8 or 10 sessions, there seemed to be no progress being made and another doctor took over the case. I repeated my fears and concerns for Neelia and eventually the doctor made arrangements for her admittance to the local children's hospital for a more comprehensive evaluation.

After Neelia spent a week at the hospital, we met with two doctors from the university hospital of psychiatry and we were given the most devastating and saddening news. Neelia now had "undifferentiated schizophrenia" and that she would need to remain at the hospital for 6 weeks in order to have her new medications balanced and more evaluations completed.

Having my daughter in the hospital for such a long time was devastating. Our life seemed to be ending and I felt completely empty. My husband worked evenings and the hospital was across the river, on the other side of the city. In spite of the difficulty, I managed to make the trip to comfort my daughter (and myself) every night. We were able to bring Neelia home on weekends and this was a nice break for everyone. Taking her back to the hospital on Sunday nights was miserable. I cried silently all the way there and loudly all the way back.

When the six weeks ended, we were referred to Dr. Robin Friedlander and the West Coast Mental Health Team. Although I felt very comfortable and reassured by their presence, I knew that the real work had just begun. At the evaluation it was confirmed that Neelia was severely mentally handicapped and that we would need as much support as possible for her. This would include providing her with a full time aide. During her transition period, Neelia had lost even her most basic skills, even skills as simple as brushing her teeth. She needed help with turning on the shower, getting dressed, changing sanitary napkins, combing her hair. She had no concept of time, money or days passing. Her eating habits became so bad that it was no longer comfortable to eat at a restaurant with her.

Things weren't easy. Some medications worked but then their beneficial effects wore off and things worsened. There were lots of negative side effects. Neelia would suddenly awake at midnight wanting to eat as she could not understand that it was not time for breakfast. She developed "Tardive Dyskineisa" and sometimes I wondered if the neighbors were concerned about her "funny walk". Eventually I overcame my own insecurities, met with a few people on our street and told them about Neelia's many problems. Most people expressed sympathy and genuine understanding but one person actually suggested that our family might have done something bad in a past life to have this "punishment" bestowed upon us.

The mental health team was very supportive. Neelia had an art therapist, a child psychologist who visited every week, and an advocate support at school meetings. Any recommendations made by the health nurse were followed. Neelia also had a life support worker to help her function at school.

In spite of her progress, Neelia suffered tremendously. She was considered "different or weird", she had no friends and she was teased endlessly. (To this day she still has bad memories of the teasing at school!)

Life at home was not good either. Neelia lacked reasoning, so she was extremely frustrated and I suffered the brunt of those frustrations. At times she would scratch me, punch me or pull my hair. The next day, she would not recall the violence. She often destroyed things around the house. Before and after her menstrual period she would express feelings of wanting to kill herself. At the worst times, including her trying to strangle me, we had to call 911 for assistance. I became so petrified of my own daughter that often I would just crouch in a corner during her attacks.

Finally I realized that I needed to take control of the situation. I began to address her in a much firmer voice and act more assertively towards her. Even though this action was not a complete deterrent, the instances became more infrequent and I began to regain some control. At this point it had been almost eleven years that we had been dealing with a child who was not only mentally handicapped but also mentally ill.

After finishing High School, Neelia began to attend a regular day program. Things began to improve but we had some initial issues to work through. After receiving the services of a behavior therapist, we found that the problems could be resolved. This therapy was very helpful and even the disruptive behavior at home was disappearing. Neelia made a conscious effort to control her temper. She would even vocalize her realization that even though something made her angry, she should not explode. She would say, "Mom I should not get mad. What for!" I would reassure her and praise her for her appropriate decision and self control.

She regained many personal life skills, even relearning to dress herself. In fact, she became very clothes conscious. The day program provided access to music through CDs, radio and the occasional live show. Neelia loves music and recognizes songs, even memorizes the words. This music access helped return her to her former gentler self.

Unfortunately, this new progress made Neelia very aware of her disability. Her perception was strong enough that she expressed her dismay at what she sees as her shortcomings. She told us that she wished she were not handicapped because she could not make friends.

Thankfully, Neelia did begin to meet many elderly disabled people on her outings. It gives her such a feeling of worth and accomplishment to help them with their needs. These individuals enjoy having Neelia's attention and she enjoys talking to them.

All these years, in my dedication to Neelia, I had been neglecting my son. On weekends he would simply disappear and sometimes I didn't realize that he wasn't home until he returned Sunday night. This situation caused a great rift in our relationship and, even though he didn't vocalize his own concerns nor complain about the attention directed to Neelia, he eventually broke down. He confided that he was petrified that he might also get a mental illness. He had been holding these feelings inside for so long and I had not had the time to recognize those fears nor to re-assure or comfort him. I had been attending a very positive, helpful support group for parents and suggested that he join the group for siblings. He chose not to participate but I am still hoping that one day he will become more involved with Neelia's life. At least our own relationship has become stronger and I know in my heart that he loves his sister very much.

Throughout the years there have been many times when I felt that I had been pushed to my limit, times I felt I simply could not do any more. Each time, I gathered my strength and mustered on. I always felt that I could never give up on my daughter, never turn her care over to other people. I dreaded the possibility of having to make a decision regarding a change in her living arrangements.

In 2004, that decision was taken out of my hands.

Although she had told us that she was feeling depressed again, Neelia was still coping on a daily basis. She mentioned several times that she felt like killing herself but we had remained optimistic that these thoughts would pass. We were proven wrong one horrible day in December when our daughter simply walked in front of a moving suv.

Neelia is now residing in a safe and secure group home. She comes home to us every weekend and, after a year of transition, she seems to be doing well. She is also in a new day program that is designed more to her needs and this is also working out well.

Our daughter has become a very sensitive 24 year old, always concerned about the needs of others. At her new program there is a young man who can not speak and Neelia told me that this makes her very sad. I responded by telling her how much more fortunate she was and that we could all be thankful for so many things. I believe this so much.

I know that Neelia will continue to blossom and I am very proud of her ongoing progress. She is learning to play the guitar, is watching her weight and health and she regularly swims 40 laps in the pool. She has even mastered the computer.

Neelia has a genuine unconditional love for others and always expresses her great desire to help those less able than herself. The staff members at her day program love her. They describe our daughter as a wonderful human being and we couldn't agree more!

WILL

Will is now in his forties.

I first met Will and his mom about 12 years ago. Will had life-long learning and hearing problems, but was a well liked, hardworking, responsible individual. He lived independently and always seemed to have a smile on his face.

In spite of a very supportive network of family and friends, Will suffers from bouts of anxiety and depression, originally brought on by multiple and sequential stressful events in his life. As his mother notes, there were so many things in his life that he had no control over!

Although Will's mood changes could normally be quite incapacitating, they have been very responsive to treatment.

—RF

WILL'S STORY

My youngest child, Will, was born in 1960 and we were over-joyed to welcome a fourth healthy son to the family.

When he was five months old, Will caught German Measles. He was very sick for a week and the illness left him with impaired hearing and crossed eyes.

Later, Will developed an eating problem and he stopped growing at a healthy rate. Often he would wake up during the night with long episodes of crying and screaming. At 15 months, he contracted chicken pox and, once more, was a very sick toddler. At 19 months and again at 24 months, Will had surgery to correct his eyes. After his visual problems had been corrected with surgery, we addressed the hearing loss.

The legendary actor, Spencer Tracy, had helped establish an innovative clinic in Los Angeles (The John Tracy Clinic) after his own son was born without hearing. Will and I spent six weeks at this learning centre and I learned "how to effectively teach a child how to speak". During those six short weeks, we discovered that Will had an exceptional gift for lip reading. The unique speech lessons continued throughout Will's school years—at home and with a speech therapist three times a week—and his regular activities were encouraged enormously by his big brothers.

When he was 3, Will had a second bout of German Measles. The high fever he experienced resulted in a session of convulsions and he was hospitalized.

During these years, Will's father was not only supporting the family but he was also instrumental in the founding and growth of the Vancouver Oral Centre, a place where all families could get information and assistance. (Throughout the years, both my husband

and I were very active members of the Society for Children with a Hearing Handicap.)

From 1963 to 1966 Will attended preschool at the hospital and then moved to a regular school that had a special teacher for the deaf. In spite of being hospitalized many times, experiencing recurring seizures and undergoing numerous EEGs and other tests, Will was a very happy boy. He was always smiling and singing.

Will's problems with his ears and eyes continued and, most likely as a result of all the numerous invasive procedures, he did develop an overwhelming fear of hospitals and needles. (He screamed so loudly when school nurses were giving tetanus shots to all the students, he was made exempt from the immunization program!)

In 1967, Will had his tongue clipped due to dental concerns.

To add insult to injury, Will's problems became compounded when he contracted Acute Infantile Hemiplegia. This viral attack left him with right side paralysis and some degree of brain damage. This new setback was the worst point of his life and we all became even more determined to make his life as normal and fulfilled as possible. Once again, his brothers pitched in with enthusiasm. On Halloween our eldest son carried Will through the neighborhood on his shoulders to be sure his little brother wouldn't miss out on the trick-or-treat experience.

Will continued to persevere and managed to complete elementary school. Moving on to high school was more intimidating as he initially felt insecure being surrounded by all the "big kids". Eventually he attended the assisted classes with enthusiasm. After school, his life was pretty much the same as any other boy. He had a paper route and learned to garden. Friends regularly took him to the local pool and he learned to swim. He was always happy and friendly to everyone he met there.

At his graduation, although he couldn't hear a word that was spoken, Will understood the honor of being presented with an award. He happily went onstage to shake his Principal's hand and accept a trophy for "the boy who always has a smile on his face".

In 1979, a unique employment agency found Will a job at a Pub close to our home. He did gardening and cleaning for them five mornings a week, sometimes working more if there was a need to shovel snow in the winter. Once, as a joke, someone at work dared him to grow a beard. The joke was on them, though, as the family gene pool enables our men to sprout lush beards almost overnight. (This little joke also worked to Will's advantage. Since he is only 5 feet tall and slightly built, the beard made him look older and more formidable and he has been sporting a beard to this day.)

Will's regular employment continued for almost 11 years and he felt stable and secure.

In 1990, Will's life changed quickly and drastically. First, the pub got new management and professional cleaners were hired. Will's job became redundant and he became unemployed. He felt rejected and was devastated. That same year two of his brothers got married and he no longer had those "best buddies" living at home. Then his two "best girl" friends got married and he became an outsider in their lives. The final blow came when his father had a heart attack. It became more than Will could handle and he became very depressed.

A consultant with the Western Institute for the Deaf, as well as a neurophysiologist, were consulted and their conclusion as that ". . . has all the safety qualities, he is high functioning" and that we should ". . . accept him as he is". We already knew that. What we didn't know was how to help him out of his slump.

Will was living with one brother, was doing lots of gardening, and was working for another brother at a job site. He was keeping busy, but he just wasn't his old happy self. When Will wasn't happy, everyone felt the impact, especially me. When he was going through difficult times we would be up all night. If he did manage to fall sleep, he would be up again at 4 or 5 am.

It took some time, but the employment agency was eventually able to find Will a permanent job at a sponsored resource centre. When his cousin moved to the city and offered to share an apartment, things really began to look a lot brighter.

Then, suddenly, my husband had a second stroke. His deteriorating health made it necessary to move from our family's house into a small condo. The change in his home-base on top of his father's poor health became a major source of distress for Will and suddenly I found myself responsible for two people in crisis.

Will had a great deal of trouble lip reading and understanding his dad's speech after the last stroke and, with his own new limitations, my husband no longer had as much patience with Will. When our third son got married, Will no longer had a sibling at home to run interference. He took every chance he had to go to our cottage. He could be alone there, grow sweet peas and dahlias in his garden and enjoy bonfires whenever he wished.

After his cousin got married, Will lived alone for the first time and we had new challenges.

My own stress continued to grow but fortunately, I was able to make an appointment with an experienced and sympathetic social worker. At the meeting, Will was very anxious and he couldn't sit still. The social worker not only watched Will's agitated movements; she also listened attentively to my concerns. She acted swiftly and requested an immediate psychiatric assessment for Will. In a very short time we were able to meet with Dr. Robin Friedlander at the West Coast Mental Health Clinic in Port Coquitlam. Dr. Friedlander was said to be one of the very few psychiatrists who had a special interest and dedication to patients who not only had a mental handicap but who also had developed a mental illness.

Although I went on the first visit with a certain amount of skepticism, I was nonetheless hoping for some real help for Will. To say that I was happy with the results would be a huge understatement.

When Will's medications were changed to a regime of Effexor and Risperdal, the reaction was immediate. Although it seems near miraculous and hard to believe, the fact is that within mere days the old "happy Will" was back. He became a calmer, more content young man and I was able to effectively handle our home and my husband's daily needs.

Although Will wasn't living with me any longer, his stressful moments still affected my sleep. When he couldn't sleep or when he would wake up in the middle of the night, he would get up, come over to my condo and wake me so we could talk. We would talk for hours as I tried to calm him down. He would ask the same things over and over and over:

Am I sick in the head?

Am I going to die?

Am I going to live?

Why am I upset?

Is it okay if I don't know what to do?

Can I turn everything off?

Are you okay?

Why do I get mad?

Whose fault is this?

Why am I unhappy?

Will I get better?

Why am I so frustrated?

Why is it so hard to get going?

He would cry; he would shake; he was scared, he couldn't sit still. He followed me around the rooms with his attention span gone. Then he would tell me to just "forget it" and we would sit and worry, worry, worry together as I tried my best to knock all the soldiers down.

Our annual meetings with Dr. Friedlander remain my lifeline.

Will is now 45 years old and still living on his own. He does all his own shopping and cleaning, knows all the bus routes, pays his own rent and does his own banking. Although he receives government funding monthly and BC Housing subsidizes his rent, his stretched finances periodically become an issue. His recreational life is assisted by a weekly outing with an experienced support worker who helps him plan interesting and affordable excursions.

I do believe he manages very well in spite of his limitations and handicaps.

He has 3 wonderful brothers (with families) and lots of great friends and relatives. He works two or three days a week, volunteers at a local bowling alley as well as at a daycare centre for dogs where, as he puts it, "You don't have to lip read to understand dogs"!

Will has friends on a nearby island that he visits twice a year. He travels on his own, taking a bus to the terminal, then a ferry and another bus to their home. Although their daughter is no longer his "best girl", her parents remain very special to him.

ADDITIONAL PERSONAL OBSERVATIONS ABOUT MY SON:

Will needs structure. He does not have the capacity for change and can't deal with concepts such as time

Will's world is limited because he can't hear or communicate well

We can't tell Will everything.

Will needs social contact.

Will has the same rights as any other adult.

Will feels tension from all of us.

Will's "acting out" is how we all feel at times.

Will needs to feel safe.

Will's emotions have nothing to do with his deafness.

Will feels the same emotions that we all do.

Will's very sensitive and his ability to handle his emotions is very fragile.

When Will feels that his world has fallen apart, he feels very frightened and becomes very dramatic.

Will was not born with mental retardation. His illnesses left him brain damaged and I believe there is a difference.

There are so many things that Will can not control in his life. This is very frustrating for him and very exhausting for me. The emotional support he requires, combined with the lack of sleep, leaves me feeling drained. At times, the worry for my son's future can be overwhelming. Although Will is "almost" independent, his needs remain constant in my life and it is so important to know that dependable, professional support is always just a phone call away.

ROBBIE

Robbie is now in his thirties.

He has an inherited genetic syndrome called Tuberous Sclerosis which causes both intellectual disability and seizures.

Although I am the doctor, Robbie has actually taught me a few things. When I first met him, he was abusing street drugs and had developed psychosis. When the risk of increasing brain damage from continued substance abuse was explained to him, Robbie simply stopped taking drugs. Although he still experienced a craving for drugs for 5 years, he only relapsed once.

The Special Olympics movement deserves some credit for Robbie's success. They offered him a healthy outlet for his energy and directed his single-mindedness into positive goals.

Robbie was one of the speakers at the conference in 2004 and he received a standing ovation!

—RF

ROBBIE'S STORY

Robbie was our planned middle child and was born in 1971. My pregnancy went smoothly and the Caesarean birth was uneventful. My son was deemed to be normal and healthy with very active tear ducts being the only noticeable distinction.

When my father visited for the first time, as gently as he could, and being as protective and loving as possible, he said he felt there was something wrong with my baby. He had seen the same look in the infant eyes of my younger brother Ken who was diagnosed with Cerebral Palsy. Shocked, then furious, I told him he was wrong and ordered him out of my house.

Just before our scheduled post-natal check-up, Robbie's tears stopped flowing. Our family physician noticed that the tear ducts were swollen shut and immediately slit them open with a razor. Although this action was horrifying enough to me, at that moment I became terrified that something may actually be wrong with my son and expressed these fears. The physician assured me that having sealed tear ducts was not an unusual occurrence and that I shouldn't be overly concerned. Nonetheless, it was difficult to shake my uneasy feeling. I had an overwhelming sense that my father may have been right. Maybe Robbie didn't have Cerebral Palsy but I began to sense the same "differences" that my father had noticed. From that moment I began watching for more signs.

By two and a half months, Robbie had more than doubled his birth weight. He slept soundly and snored as loudly as an old man. His ears produced an unusually large amount of wax despite daily cleansing and I mentioned this to our physician. Again, he wasn't concerned so I didn't worry either. As a young mother, I didn't have the confidence to question his professional opinion.

When Robbie was four months old, he began to lose circulation if he sat in his baby seat for as little as half an hour. Initially, Steve and I would rub his little arm and leg until the colour returned but, after several of these episodes, we felt that something was definitely wrong. When we took Robbie to the doctor, he said we were over-reacting; that he had never observed any unusual symptoms. We deferred to his opinion and just made sure that Robbie spent shorter times in a sitting position.

Within a month, two more strange incidences occurred. One day, as I was feeding Robbie, he leaned his forehead to press it against mine. This was a sweet gesture of affection so I sat still and let him continue with his "forehead embrace". Suddenly I became so dizzy I fainted just long enough to land my cheek in his bowl of cereal. Then, on another day, I was carrying Robbie up the stairs. When he gently pressed his head against mine, I became woozier with each step I took and my vision became cloudy. Fortunately, my 3 year old was at the top of the stairs and was able to grab Robbie because I suddenly lost control and slid all the way down.

My mother listened to all our concerns and strange incidents with Robbie and advised us to consult a specialist. She had gone through so much with Ken's CP, especially in his infancy, and she urged us to seek more experienced medical help. She was adamant about us demanding a second opinion, but I decided to give our doctor another chance.

One day (in his fifth month) Robbie was bouncing in his exerciser when he had a seizure. I'd never seen a seizure before and the powerful image of my baby losing control of his eyes, his head fallen over to one side and his arms hanging limply while his shoulders shook like a rag doll was terrifying. His strong little legs that, just moments before, had been joyously pushing his toes against the floor were now gyrating uncontrollably and I rushed to call for help.

Although once again the doctor did not believe a word I said, he agreed to see us within hours. Robbie suffered a half dozen more seizures on the bus ride to the office but didn't have any once we arrived for our appointment. Since the doctor didn't personally observe any seizure activity, he dismissed the episodes I described as being a reaction to the heat of the day or possible dehydration. Days later, when the seizures returned, my newly-found indignation met his pride full-on and I finally demanded a referral to a paediatric specialist.

Robbie had seven seizures in the paediatrician's office and the man went to work like a mad scientist. It seemed strange that anyone would be so pleased to see the onset of seizures but, by being able to observe Robbie during his seizures and perform his examination under these extreme conditions, he was better able to assess the situation. Robbie was admitted to hospital immediately.

After a short visit home to comfort our other son, I returned to the hospital to find an almost-unrecognizable baby. His beautiful blonde hair had been shaved and his head was stained with a dirty-looking orange smear of antiseptic. He was so traumatized that he couldn't focus. His eyes seemed lifeless and he was completely unresponsive. If I hadn't believed my father's premonition before, I certainly did now.

On the second day, Robbie had a spinal tap. He didn't cry much during the session but he was in pain for quite awhile. When I saw the raised vessels on his head and his tiny temples pounding so hard I regretted ever bringing him to hospital. Robbie always had one of us with him during the next, most surreal ten days I've ever experienced. A famous American brain surgeon was visiting and he agreed to examine Robbie.

Although several days passed and the specialist was long gone, we received no information. An understanding nurse, after much pressure and pleading from us, would only say that Robbie had Infant Petit Mal Seizures; that he may grow out of them, and in the meantime they could probably be controlled with Phenobarbital.

It was much later that we finally received the diagnosis. Our son was developmentally impaired and epileptic. Robbie looked so perfect, so beautiful and he had such a sweet disposition that my husband and I were in shock to hear such devastating news.

During his first year, Robbie and I attended weekly physio and occupational therapy lessons to strengthen his limbs and stimulate his sensations on his right side. We hoped to help develop both sides of his body while the seizures were being controlled by medication. About this time, he began to express frustration with his inability to verbally communicate. He used screaming to vent anger and to let us know when he didn't understand us.

Curiously, Robbie could walk very well at thirteen months but then his walking deteriorated and his ankles began to turn outward. The same tight-lipped neurologist who made the initial diagnosis examined him and, after an x-ray, he scheduled Robbie for a hip operation.

Before we had a date set for the surgery, we attended the hospital's yearly "specialist event". Teaching specialists, along with their numerous residents, examined one patient after another and then gave assessments on conditions and progress. It was very tiring being asked the same questions over and over and, after a few hours, I felt like a lab rat. Finally, our own neurologist arrived with his students. After describing the situation of "the case", he coolly announced that he was surprised that Robbie could even sit up, let alone ever walk, considering his diagnosis. Shocked, hurt and confused, I angrily reacted by asking him why he wanted to put Robbie through the pain of hip surgery if he felt my son would never walk anyway. Red-faced with embarrassment, the doctor just turned his back and walked out.

He never did apologize for his inconsideration. Thankfully, our physiotherapist had shown us exercises to strengthen Robbie's legs and we faithfully followed her directions. We were determined to help our son in any way we could.

One night, as I was hanging upside down off the side of the sofa, playing with the kids, my husband told me to watch Robbie's face. Steve took my place and I watched both of them. Robbie was a natural mimic with a "rubber face" and usually kept us laughing. This time we weren't laughing at all. Robbie would frown when we would smile and smile when we would frown. Was he trying to be funny by doing the opposite of what we expected or was it an inappropriate reaction from his eyes, his drugs or his brain? If his eyesight made things appear upside down, that might account for his poor balance while walking. He had been falling down after a few steps and then reverting to crawling in a drunken manner but we really didn't know where to look for answers. We had lost confidence in our doctors, especially when we discovered that the paediatrician had been prescribing too large a dose of Phenobarbital for almost six months!

Soon Robbie exhibited another unusual behaviour. Just before he experienced one of his seizures, he would stop whatever he was doing and quietly sit down on the floor. He looked like he was listening to something or waiting for something to happen. Then, with a determined face, he'd make fists, get into a furious state and pound the floor. Eventually he would go limp and his body would be taken over by the seizure. Robbie continued to handle his episodes this way so we always knew when one was coming. I would hold him safely until it passed and time the duration so I could see if the seizures were changing at all. They seemed to remain constant, lasting no more than a minute and a half and having no apparent pattern.

After awhile, Robbie seemed to be able to delay the onset of a seizure for a few moments by angrily concentrating. As time went on, the anger seemed to change to a determined focus as he tried to stave off the episode. I wasn't happy with Robbie's numbed state of mind though. I began to secretly shave fine dust from his tablets, a tiny bit each day or so. As there were no ill effects, I continued this weaning method until he was drug-free. By age two, not only had his seizures stopped but he was more alert and active.

When Robbie was five, we were finally told that he also had Tuberous Sclerosis. What I knew about Robbie's fragile health in the beginning was already overwhelming for a young mother so perhaps it was better that he wasn't hindered with the added diagnosis much earlier. Five years of developing deep love for him and growing in confidence in my parenting skills made it easier to receive the prognosis: "He'll live to the age of somewhere between fifteen and thirty and I wouldn't expect much of him if I were you. Something janitorial maybe. Can't be helped." Remembering the words still breaks my heart.

Not all doctors are true healers and they all must work within the framework of the knowledge they received in their training. In 1980, when I searched for information on Tuberous Sclerosis at a medical university library, I found only one half page in one reference book and a column and a half in another. In an ironic twist of fate, in 1997 I was also diagnosed with Tuberous Sclerosis. I was 47. Personally I'm glad I didn't know earlier as I truly don't know if I would have unintentionally limited myself. Now, of course, I share a unique understanding, perspective and experience with my son that may have influenced his progress in many ways.

In his adolescence, Special Olympics became a new opportunity for Robbie. Team sports did not give him the challenges he was looking for and this wonderful organization instilled faith in his gifts and encouraged his potential to use them. Like most people, Robbie functions best in an atmosphere of love. He is the most devoted person anyone could ever know. He is so appreciative to family, friends and anyone who assists him for the betterment of his life. (Even before he had the example of Special Olympics, Robbie always encouraged others.)

He regularly visits friends with special needs and he has encouraged them to practice meditation by showing them basic techniques. He has the ability to recognize depression in his friends. He warns them about junk food and he takes them out for walks so they won't live like hermits.

It is one of his natural gifts to be kind and to share his wisdom and experience with others who are categorized as being "different."

In his teens, Robbie experienced times of deep depression where he couldn't even leave his home. With depression came his tendency to obsess. Perhaps because he was so lonely or perhaps because he needed an outlet for sexual expression, Robbie experimented with cross- dressing. His frustrations turned his emotions more and more inward until he actually endangered himself socially, mentally and physically by venturing out to explore his options.

There is enough dysfunction and danger in the homosexual world without the added handicap of a learning disability. I don't know if his actions showed he was being brave or naïve, but I believe my son deserves credit for wanting to investigate his choices. Although we understood his needs, we still were very fearful for him. It took counselling, consultations with doctors at the STD clinic, numerous discussions with his support worker (who lived above his apartment) and long talks with his older brother and me before Robbie could understand the importance of a healthy sexual attitude and lifestyle. It was frustrating and sad to witness the trials and tribulations of his journey to discover his sexual identity. It was even worse to witness the abuse he took from both men and women and we were disgusted to realize there were people depraved enough to prey on an innocent like Robbie. (The police were involved on two occasions when Robbie was seriously hurt but their seemingly indifferent response only made me question if all disabled people were so undervalued.)

My son is my favourite hero in this world because of how brave, dedicated and kind he is. I took it very seriously when we were invited to contribute to this book. Robbie is a complex man who, in spite of everything that could keep him small in this world, shines brighter the longer he remains a conscious spirit in this human experience. I often tell him that he has been my greatest teacher and that he continues to surprise me with his ability to wrap his intentions around the quality of grace. No matter what seems to be going on at the surface, Robbie is able to be intimate with the depths of life.

I dearly hope Robbie and I have touched others in a helpful way and we wish the best for all those searchers who needed to hear what we had to say.

The next section of this chapter was dictated by Robbie to his mother. She was overwhelmed by his candid honesty and willingness to share his deepest thoughts, feelings and memories. There has been minimal editing of Robbie's statement so the reader can truly appreciate the clarity of Robbie's emotions and the integrity of his character. Not many people with a history and diagnosis similar to Robbie's can express their journey so well and his contribution is gratefully recognized.

MY LIFE ACCORDING TO ROBBIE

When I was in nursery school, I thought I was in hell. I saw this whole group of kids who were all having difficulties and I was confused because some of them were deformed and they looked like monsters to me. Their faces were like cartoon characters and their voices sounded distorted and it scared the heck out of me. I thought I had a different face, a different mind. It was so odd to see this. There was no way for me to tell where I fit in to all of it. When I got off the school bus, kids would call me "retarded" or "reject". I was shocked when I first heard it. I thought that the whole entire world thought I was retarded. My mom used to tell people that I just took a little longer to learn than other kids. The teachers treated everyone that was slower the same. When I was a child I didn't know if they expected the same things from me or not. They got impatient with me once in a while. One time they locked me in a room by myself for having a temper tantrum. From the way I remember the room my mother said this would have to be before I was four.

When I was small it felt pretty normal playing with other kids. I have a brother two years older and a sister two years younger. All along I hung out with my brother so his friends became my friends. This became difficult for me when my brother went to high school. At this time I was living with my dad and his new wife and a few times I brought a friend home. This was difficult for my stepmother because my friends were not as high functioning as me and one was a brat and the other couldn't communicate very well and he was not very social. My stepmother did not really like to have my friends from my school visit my home. It was too much trouble to deal with them. My brothers told me that it was better to hang out with them because it would improve my vocabulary and they taught me how to count up to one thousand and they encouraged me to read The Hobbit. I thought it was hard at first but I read it.

If I were to say which primary school was the best for me I would say it was in my eleventh year. A van picked us up and it was a one hour drive twice a day. There were more high functioning students like me which meant I could talk with them. We did math, played in the gym and sang songs. We had enough students to put together a bowling team and competed with another Special Needs school in another town.

The only sad thing about that time was that I got into an argument with a bigger boy when I was playing street hockey and he called me retarded. I hadn't heard that in a long time and it really offended me. My brothers were not around to defend me and I got really scared and I had to back down. After that I was mad. A couple years later when my parents bought a house in the country I experienced name calling again and this time it was by a number of boys. I was surprised because one of them was a friend of my stepbrother. He had been nice to me when I was with my stepbrother. The boys got very abusive with words and when I told my brothers, we equipped ourselves with some hockey sticks planning to knock some manners into them. Luckily a man from the village had the good sense to change our minds.

My stepbrother and I were inspired by the Karate Kid movie and we joined a karate club together. Jason lasted a short time and I stayed on. I really liked the moves. Inside I was still fearful about being hurt and I felt I didn't have the guts. The instructors tried to show me the techniques properly used in sparring but I got hit a lot. I was very strong, but I didn't believe in myself even though I progressed to a purple belt. When I moved to Vancouver at twenty-three I changed to Kung Fu. Martial arts were in my life in a new way. My instructor saw great potential in me and gave me confidence. I know learning meditation and practising Chi Gong gave me peace, awareness, trust in what I know and the ability to carry it out. I had always been more afraid that I would hurt someone else if I got too angry even when I did Karate. A new teacher plus my new techniques of calming myself gave me control.

When I moved to Vancouver, I was looking for friendships and I began with the people I met while going to school. I felt pretty helpless to make the right choices of proper friends. Unfortunately I started experimenting with drugs and hanging out with people who did too. I made a choice pretty quick to stop hanging out with one guy because he smoked pot and pot made me feel paranoid. My other friend lived in a place that had lots of small apartments and he was friends with a lot more people. At least I thought they were friends. Those men used us for our money and we got into drinking and doing crack and LSD. This created frustrations and bad feelings in my house because I spent my rent and I was lying and ruining trust. My martial arts suffered because I couldn't perform as well. I started having paranoid dreams and these dreams made my waking state distorted and fearful.

My interest was beginning to go toward acting. I don't know how I did it but I managed to learn lines and take guitar lessons as well. Then it all became too much for me to keep up. Something had to give, so I let go of Kung Fu. I was getting hit in the head too often and I felt in danger. I was worried after I saw my CT Scan of my head and I saw all the tubers. I already knew that a bad impact could make my condition worse. Then the specialist said that I was taking too many chances and an impact sport could cause serious complications. His advice plus actually seeing an image of my brain and the many cysts made it easier to give up drugs.

Crack was the one that took the longest. I thought I ended it in 1998, but then I tried it again once in 2000. I haven't had any since then but in 2005, I went for counselling because I felt an experience of craving in my throat and chest. I went to a Dual Diagnosis Centre where I listened to a talk about how crack causes Parkinson's disease and paranoia. I learned that the craving I was having was caused by the nerve damage of doing the drug. The counsellor and doctor told me I was a very lucky person to have stopped because I could have died or, worse, I could have been crippled or become a low functioning person.

I realize, because I am an athlete, that with all my training and competitions I can experience a natural high. Even when I think about it I get excited when I imagine doing my best. My best as it turns out is when I am doing individual competition. Sure I'm on the

Vancouver snow shoeing team and have been on the swim team for years but where I can really focus is on the individual sports of power lifting and running. These two sports I can use my Chi Gong energy and state of mind. Part of it is for healing, and the rest for strength, self awareness, balance, joy, endurance, focus, visualizing, and for staying in a state of peace and dedication. Drugs are like sugar. A drug dissolves like sugar and when it's gone you have nothing left and you're poor, stuck in a bottomless pit.

All my life my family and friends would tell me to stop repeating things. I just couldn't help myself. I had a one track mind. Obsessing about my interests or any powerful emotional experience was altered quite a bit by combining sports and meditation in a routine way. It made me focus and I felt smarter because I could read better. I started writing my own music and songs on the guitar and I felt fluent in martial arts.

I could have used this confidence when I was going to the life skills school the year before because focusing was difficult for me there. A psychologist had tested me and I was very upset by what he wrote. He said I could only read at a grade six level and that I was retarded. That hurt me. I was trying to convince others I wasn't retarded. I had been raised to believe I was high functioning and my brothers told me I'd be able to learn when I got older. My interview with that man and what he wrote bothered me even more because he tried to limit my chances. I have proven him wrong because I have never stopped reading and learning and I have a real interest in learning other languages. From people I work with and from using language CDs, I am even learning Mandarin, Cantonese and Vietnamese.

I do have to mention that the neurologist helped me in 1998 by prescribing Gabapentan when I was getting so angry. Sometimes I broke things and punched holes in doors and walls and I yelled at my priority care worker. The doctor felt I may be having seizures so tiny you can't measure them on a graph and that these may have been making me feel confused, irritable and impatient. Because I wasn't totally off street drugs then and because my diet included many of the things the other doctor warned me against using in anything but moderation, I can't say I realized the full benefit of the prescription.

We had been calling my reactions to food "allergies" and the doctor said they were more than likely just "sensitivities". He laughed when he said that me and my mom were just more sensitive than most people to being poisoned by food additives, pesticides, fertilizers, colorants, and preservatives. People like us experience interference in our mind and body and emotions from taking in the chemicals that don't seem to bother other people as much. He recommended going organic as much as possible. I told him I got angry when I ate potatoes. He asked if tomatoes and peppers bothered me as well. My mom has a real problem with potatoes too. If she eats them a couple of times in a row she gets very agitated and short tempered.

It was frustrating trying to eat what I should because, at first, my priority care worker didn't believe I had a sensitivity problem. My mother disagreed a lot with her about this and it made things tense between all of us. In my last year there, my worker noticed my feet and toes were in such a bad state with discoloured thick nails and dry cracked skin, so she finally agreed with Mom that I had Candida. She found lots of information and advice on the Internet and created a diet to help me through it. She would get angry at me for buying chips and pop and coffee. Eating the wrong things made me full of mucus. I would regurgitate and have a heavy, bloated tummy as well as acids burning my throat. I tried to be moderate, but I kept craving those things, especially coffee. My mother and my worker would talk a lot about my anger resurfacing again.

I was also hearing voices and having fear about being hurt by people in the neighbourhood. It scared the heck out of my worker when I cried out in the middle of the night especially when her husband was away. She took me to a psychiatrist and he put me on Risperidol. My mother got upset because she felt it was because of my diet that I had mental imbalances and she felt my worker didn't act on it soon enough and that's why the situation got worse. My worker knew how mom felt about drug treatment and that is why she didn't tell her about the decision about the Risperidol. It didn't help that Mom felt that my worker and me had a roller coaster relationship, one that I had out grown. I was frustrated with some areas of my life and wanted to be more independent, and my worker had the kind of personality that made me always on the defensive. It never seemed to be peaceful any more. Around this time she was pregnant and once the baby came, the situation escalated to the point I had to move out.

A huge part of my deteriorating health was due to being lonely for a sweetheart. I ate things I shouldn't so I could feel like I was treating myself. If I went over to see friends, I would treat them too. Over the years, I have had girlfriends but then I became interested in men as well. My experiences in homosexuality have not been as rewarding as I had hoped. Ever since I was in nursery school I recall being attracted to unusual people because I didn't really know who I was. Besides this, from a very early age, I had a fascination for accessories. It was a point of humour in my family that, when I was only four, I turned up wearing a pair of lime green goggles to my uncle's wedding. By the time I was five I was trying on my mother's lingerie. I was just a kid who liked to dress up and the only guilt I felt was that I was invading someone else's property and privacy. When I think about this I realize that I never really stopped trying on women's clothes and I recall doing it every few years or so. It got more frequent as I became a teenager. Once, my brothers caught me creating a bust-line by stuffing socks into my shirt. Of course, back then, I just took a ribbing for that but more recently my brother informed everyone that I have been cross dressing in public. My family said there is nothing wrong with it but I know they worry that I'll get attacked by gay bashers.

I have had sexual counselling with two different counsellors. One said cross dressing didn't mean anything. Both straights and gays do it. He suggested that I play it safe and stay indoors. The other one gave me information about the types of sexual activities that indicated if a person was gay or straight. I was struggling with my sexual identity. Counselling didn't really answer it for me but it gave me the chance to explore my thoughts and talk openly. I also got a lot of advice from the many gay/bi/trannies who only wanted to take advantage of me. Occasionally I would meet a genuine person who could teach me things I needed to know. I tried to meet men at bars but I am not a very good drinker. When I drank I made some pretty dangerous decisions. After a few of these mistakes, my family and care worker were in a panic. My brother took me to the STD clinic for an AIDS test. It finally started sinking in how bad it could have turned out and I made a decision to protect myself. My experience with gay men has taught me that because I want a special relationship with protected sex, real love is a lot harder to find.

Right now I'm in a new living situation that gives me lots of freedom. I have a male room mate who challenges me from time to time with his unpredictable temper and jealousy. I enjoy the company of the various workers at our home, the friendly neighbourhood and the convenience of the gym near by. I'm still getting used to being mindful of someone else's disability. Watching my roommate struggle with his emotions reminds me of when I had problems in this area—especially when he wrecks my stuff. Now I know how others must have felt when I got mad and broke their things.

My near future takes me to climb Mt. Kilimanjaro and then I will compete in the Special Olympic Nationals for Power Lifting. I feel grounded because I am balanced in my life and I feel excited because I get to have new adventures where I can experience my very best.

ROSEANNE

Roseanne is now 40.

She is one of the few people I know with an intellectual disability who has qualified for a driver's license!

As Roseanne's birth mother had schizophrenia, she was unable to look after her baby and she put her into foster care. Roseanne was eventually adopted by her foster mother, an incredible woman who has successfully fostered numerous children in her lifetime.

About 5 years ago, after being treated for a psychotic depression, Roseanne was referred to our team for follow-up.

Roseanne still lives with her mother who is now in her 80's. She has written her own story.

—RF

ROSEANNE'S STORY

Forty years ago, I was born with developmental disabilities. When I was just six weeks old I was placed in a foster home. This was supposed to be a temporary placement and the foster family was told I would be transferred to a hospital institution within a week. That never happened. I stayed with my foster family and just before I started school they adopted me permanently.

When I was 5 years old I went to our neighborhood school on the special "bunny bus". The children at the school poked fun at me and called it the "Nutty Bus". When I had plastic surgery on my ears and had to go to school with my head bandaged for a few days, they were mean and said "Oh! They gave her some new brains". I still remember it.

I was put in a regular grade one class when I was six years old but it was stressful for me dealing with all the so-called normal children. When it was time to go to secondary school, I went into a "special class" where I did very well and was "top dog on the totem pole". Finally, I was accepted and I did very well, especially at sewing. After being in that class for 3 years, I realized that I would never graduate and be able to get a job unless something changed. My mother took me and some of my sewing over to the school board and showed them just what some of the developmentally delayed students could do. They were impressed enough to give us the address of a place that made ski wear. I had never even seen a power sewing machine let alone use one but I learned quickly. I was the only "special" worker but things worked out well because the other ladies were all Chinese. I didn't know what they were saying so nothing could hurt me. I stayed at that job until the company went bankrupt.

That didn't stop me. Soon I was working in a veterinary hospital in the morning and a doggie day care in the afternoon. I was managing my life very well and even got my drivers license. When I wasn't working, I was enjoying figure skating and horseback riding and my family life was a happy one.

In my early 30's, the bottom dropped out of everything. The doctor at the veterinary hospital moved to the USA and I no longer had my stable job. Then one of my brothers died. It seemed too much to bear.

I started to think that people were spying on me. I heard voices. One night I started screaming because I was certain that I was hearing the devil telling me to do real bad things. It was very frightening to me and to my family. My mom and sister took me to the hospital where I stayed for 3 months and was diagnosed with manic depression. Mom and my sister and brother came to see me every day. We would play pool or do puzzles. I was seeing a good psychiatrist and other therapists and counselors and they all really helped me get better.

Once my new medications seemed to be working, I was able to come back home.

Although I couldn't remember very much, I did remember my bank number and my car license number. I was managing much better. The voices in my head were gone but some things made me very sad. I could not go horseback riding or figure skating because of the medications. The worst thing was that I couldn't drive my car. Because of the side effects of the medications, I spent most of the day sleeping and gained a lot of weight.

I began regular visits with the West Coast Mental Health Support Team almost five years ago and my life has been continually improving. I sleep well and don't have any more bad dreams. I see my doctor once a month and I am much more active. I am driving my car again and I go horseback riding regularly. My figure skates didn't fit for a long time but, with a change in my medications, I am starting to lose weight and I know I'll be skating again real soon.

I am very lucky to have such a loving family and so many other caring people to help me. Now I can really look forward to getting another job working with animals and get on with my life.

SUMMARY

In this post-institutional era, it has become commonplace to read about people enjoying full lives in the community despite having intellectual disabilities. There are also stories about people who successfully live in the community with severe and persistent mental illness.

Our focus is on the lives of people who live with both mental illness and ID.

One important fact has become very evident. Untreated mental illness is the major reason for failure /breakdown of community placements for people with ID.

It is time to raise the profile of this "special needs" sub-population. It is time to make decision-makers more aware of the critical situation that exists for this group. It is time to put their needs on the "top priority" list of funding agencies.

The stories in this book are real and personal. Each is unique in its perspective. All together, the stories reveal many points for concern and discussion. To begin, we offer a brief introduction to Psychiatric diagnosis and classification.

DIAGNOSIS

A "syndrome" is a term clinicians use to refer to a collection of symptoms and signs of disease which occur together more than by chance. "Diagnosis" is the shorthand which clinicians use when referring to a particular syndrome. To be valid and useful, a diagnosis should reflect a disease process. It should also advise us about the appropriate treatment and any predictable prognosis. (long term outcome)

Some of the characteristics of mental illness overlap with the emotions and thoughts that are common to the human experience. In order for a common characteristic to be considered as a symptom of disease, the feeling or thought needs to cause significant internal distress and/or have significant adverse effects for others. The symptoms should be persistent and not just an understandable reaction to stress or loss.

Mental illness is caused by biological predisposition and adverse life experiences, certain medical problems and one's unique response to these challenges. Compared to other fields of medicine, the knowledge base in psychiatry is still fairly rudimentary. As a result, we still know little about the biological underlying causes of mental illness. What we do know is that all forms of mental illness have biological, psychological and environmental/social factors in causation. This is the "bio-psycho-social model" of mental illness.

Mental illness is divided into the following categories:
a) Disorders of development including Intellectual Disability, Autism Spectrum Disorders, ADHD and Personality Disorders.
b) Disorders of mood including Bipolar Mood Disorders and Major Depression.
c) Disorders of Anxiety including Generalized Anxiety Disorder, Panic Attacks, Phobias, Obsessive Compulsive Disorder (OCD) and Separation Anxiety.
d) Psychotic disorders including Schizophrenia and other related disorders which generally manifest in hallucinations, delusions, disorganized behavior and thinking.

When the presentation of mental illness is unusual, the suffix NOS (Not Otherwise Specified) is added onto the diagnosis. (e.g.: Mood Disorder NOS)

DSM IV is the diagnostic manual used in North America for psychiatric diagnosis. DSM IV has a multi-axial diagnostic system.

Axis I   notation of the major mental illness subtype
           (e.g. schizophrenia)
Axis II   documentation of the intellectual disability (if present) or
           serious maladaptive personality traits.
Axis III notation of medical illnesses relevant to the major mental
           illness
Axis IV   documentation of relevant psychosocial stressors.
Axis V   documenting the severity of the impact of the mental
           illness on daily functioning

The diagnoses identified in the patients described in this book are the same kinds of diagnoses found in the general population.

AXIS I DIAGNOSES (CLINICAL SYNDROME)

Autism Spectrum disorders: 6
(3 cases also have other Axis I Diagnoses)

The prevalence of autism increases inversely with the intellectual level. In other words, the lower the IQ level, the higher the rate of associated autism. This is noted most often in clinics such as our own—clinics which focus on Intellectual Disability (ID). There is far more autism (also called Autism Spectrum Disorder or Pervasive Developmental Disorder) in our patients than in the general population. In fact, the diagnosis of autism appears in almost half of the patients described in this book. This is often a "double whammy" for the parents who have already had to deal with problems in intellectual and social/ interpersonal development.

Mood disorders: 5
Mood disorder NOS: 2
Bipolar: 1

Major depression: 1
Major depression with psychotic features: 1

Psychotic disorders: 5
Schizophrenia: 2
Psychosis NOS: 3

Anxiety disorders: 2
Both have OCD

The number of NOS diagnoses noted in this summary reflects the difficulties and complexities of diagnoses in individuals with limited ability to communicate. As most of psychiatric diagnosis depends on interview with the patient, a particular skill set is needed for clinicians working in this area. More attention is required to observe signs rather than eliciting symptoms from the patient. It becomes very important to gather and check information from significant family members or caregivers. The direct interview with the patient may need to be modified by using simpler language and by having the patient's support people present in the room.

AXIS II (LEVEL OF INTELLECTUAL DISABILITY):
Borderline: 1
Mild: 4
Mild to moderate: 2
Moderate: 1
Severe: 3
Profound: 2

The patients described here reflect the full range of intellectual disability (ID).

DSM IV uses the term "Mental Retardation" to refer to people with ID. As many people with ID and their families consider this label as being pejorative, the term ID is used in this book.

85% of people with ID have mild ID. This refers to an IQ score between 55 and 70.

People with IQ less than 55 include only 15% of people with ID, but these people are far more likely to have autism and have atypical presentations of mental illness. People with IQ lower than 55 are also much more likely to have a known cause for their ID (e.g. genetic or birth injury). There is often no known cause for those people whose IQ falls in the mild range of ID. (E.g. Most people with Down syndrome have Moderate ID.)

AXIS III: (RELEVANT MEDICAL SYNDROME).

Epilepsy: 7

Genetic syndromes: 4 (Alfies, Aicardi, Tuberous Sclerosis, Rubella syndrome)

Sensory impairment: 1 (deafness)

Complications of treatment: 3 (weight gain; Tardive tremor)

Gastro esophageal reflux disease (GERD): 3

Patients with ID are far more likely to have relevant medical problems which can cause a lot of pain and distress. This may present as challenging behavior which should not be mistaken as mental illness.

There are also certain medical/neurological syndromes which are strongly associated with mental illness. One important condition that has always had a complicated relationship with mental illness is epilepsy. Certain forms of epilepsy (seizures) can cause psychosis or depression. Conversely, in some people with epilepsy, irritable moods are sometimes dramatically improved by a seizure! Although epilepsy is uncommon in the general population, about half of the patients in this book had a history of this condition.

Genetic syndromes such as Alfies, Tuberous Sclerosis, Rubella and Aicardi syndrome cause changes in the development and growth of the brain. This is the cause of the intellectual disability. The syndromes may also lead to other neurological problems such as seizures. Other bodily organs such as the heart or kidneys may also have altered growth. There may also be characteristic facial features and alterations in stature.

It is noteworthy that none of our stories feature people with Down Syndrome, by far the most commonly recognized genetic syndrome associated with ID and the most commonly known cause of ID. This omission is completely coincidental but it may be relevant.

People with Down Syndrome typically have intellectual disability associated with the abovementioned characteristic facial features and short stature. They also may have problems with body organs. (One example would be congenital heart disease.)

People with Down Syndrome are less likely to have concurrent mental illness than other individuals with the same IQ level. As well, certain forms of mental illness may be manifested in a much milder form in people with Down Syndrome. (e. g. the manic phase of bipolar mood disorder.) Conversely, certain mental health problems such as early onset Alzheimer's Disease are actually more common in people with Down Syndrome.

Although we don't know enough about the mental health characteristics of most of the other genetic syndromes associated with ID, we do know that genetic changes may affect personality and behavior. As an example, people with Down Syndrome are more likely to be stubborn and determined. People with Williams' Syndrome are typically very social and musical. People with Cornelia De Lange Syndrome are more likely to self-inflict injuries when frustrated or upset. These are called behavioral phenotypes. As we learn more about these characteristics, it should help us understand the relationship between behavioral features and mental illness in the wider population. This is an exciting field of new knowledge.

We offer the following thought for discussion: Of all people with ID, those with Down Syndrome succeed best with community living. Perhaps the behavioral phenotype and the higher risk of concurrent mental disorder of people with other forms of ID require completely different types of community living supports.

AXIS IV: (IDENTIFIABLE PSYCHOSOCIAL STRESSORS):

Loss of a loved one: 3 (Response to loss of a parent in adult years)

Bullying: 4 (in the school years)

Family burn- out: 5 (In all cases, the family burn-out was a direct consequence of ongoing, severe mental illness and the result was the need for out of home placement. All the families were stressed. We have just noted those whose internal and external resources were completely overwhelmed.)

Immigration to a new country: 3 (from South Asia, South America and Vietnam)

Parental separation: 4 (8/14 patients had the ongoing support of healthy 2- parent families prior to onset of mental illness.)

OTHER RISK FACTORS FOR MENTAL DISORDER

Mental illness commonly runs in families, reflecting both genetic predispositions as well as shared familial psychosocial stress. However, in these randomly selected stories, only one person had a first degree relative with related mental illness. This may be coincidence, but it suggests that psychosocial stressors and other genetic factors relevant to the syndrome may be more important in this specific population. In other words, both psychosocial and neurobiological factors may be even more important in the genesis of mental disorder in this particular group than in the general population.

Other biological risk factors for mental illness may include birth injury and epilepsy. These two factors probably play an important role in the increased frequency of mental illness in this population.

Because biological and psychosocial stress interact to increase risk of mental illness, it is important to always investigate stressful events in people's lives. In these stories, the most immediate precipitating cause of mental illness noted was the experience of loss. Although the loss of a loved one is part of the cycle of life, the grief and sorrow can also be a trigger to the development of a depressive illness.

In childhood and adolescence, the most important predisposing event recorded in these stories was bullying in all its toxic forms (physical violence, teasing and social exclusion).

Physical or sexual abuse by adults is also an important risk factor for mental disorder. Children and adults with ID are particularly vulnerable for this risk. Although no incidents of such abuse are recorded in this group of stories, the possibility always exists. Our book is limited to the details that the contributors themselves wished to reveal for this publication.

Another risk factor is deafness as noted in one individual. In general psychiatry hearing impairment is well known to increase risk of psychosis and paranoia. One can easily understand how this sensory deficit could predispose a person to thinking that others are talking about one in a negative way (paranoia).

This may be a clue as to why people with ID in general are more vulnerable to mental illness as compared to the general population. One theory is that the experience of ID may be likened to a huge sensory and processing deficit which slows down the thinking process as well as the integration of thoughts and senses. It may be likened to being on a fast train and watching out the window as the world flashes by. In this analogy, the world speeding past the train window would be the real world, fast paced and ever changing. A person with ID inside the train focuses on one image outside the train window (for example some cows in a farmer's field). While the person with

ID is still processing that single image, the scenery behind it has changed and the view outside would have changed to one of fields of corn and a farm house. Minutes later, the view may be that of a small town, followed shortly after that by a view of mountains. For the person with ID, only fragments of the "big picture" can be processed. Most of what they see and experience is a blur of activity. This would be like having a massive sensory deficit and may be an important factor in the increased prevalence of mental disorder.

Another issue of concern is the pressure associated with integration into community living and mainstreaming. For people with ID, growing up and trying to fit in to this complex world we share must be overwhelming, even though, with appropriate support, living in the community (most particularly with family) has radically enhanced the lives of most affected people.

Whatever the cause of mental illness, we know that risk tends to be multifactorial and it is likely that multiple biological and psychosocial risk factors are at play in any one individual.

Age of onset
Our mental health teams see both adolescents as well as adults. Although their intellectual disability was diagnosed early in childhood, one third of these patients had no serious behavioral or mental health problems prior to puberty

Living situation
Of the fourteen individuals described in this book, nine are still living at home with their natural or adopted families. Of those living outside the home, sixty percent have autism and associated severe behavioral challenges. When we measure concurrent behavioral disorders in this population, autism is the leading psychiatric disorder. These statistics are not uncommon for out- of-home placement.

Medications

The patients described in this book have serious and persistent mental illness.

If the mental illness is in remission, there still remains a high risk of relapse. It is not surprising, therefore, that all of the patients described are still taking psychiatric medications. Some of the patients are also taking anticonvulsants for treating seizures and/or certain mental disorders such as bipolar mood disorder.

Many people are reluctant to take medications for mental health problems. They may feel more comfortable taking medications for neurological disorders such as epilepsy. There seems to be a perception that neurological disorders are more "medical", whereas mental health disorders are more "in the mind" and can be controlled or contained by self will or behavioral change. The fact is that mental illness is a disorder of the mind arising in the brain.

Both brain and mind are integrally involved in the development of mental illness. It is non- holistic thinking to ignore the brain part of the equation.

To answer the age old questions regarding nature or nurture as the cause of mental illness, we would now respond with the statement that the human being is affected by both nature and nurture. Our biology and our interaction with the environment are equally important.

The study of medicine is a science, the practice of which is an art. (William Osler) This is particularly true for that part of medicine which deals with the human mind. The current state of knowledge in psychiatry guides us with regard to the art of prescribing medications. We know that a longer term of treatment is necessary for many psychotic and mood disorders. Premature discontinuation of medications may profoundly and adversely affect the outcome of the mental illness.

Treatment is more than just administering medication, but medication is the most visible treatment. Because of the higher visibility of medication, it evokes the most questions and concerns. This is understandable.

The most common response to successful treatment of the mental disorder is to leave well alone. Why stop the medication, if the patient is well? As our colleague, neurologist Michael Jones, is fond of saying: "If it ain't broke, don't fix it!" We, however, usually recommend a slow tapering of the medications after a period of a year of remission of symptoms. Our aim is to determine if patients actually need to stay on the full dose of medication long term or if they can manage on a lower dose. Families invariably don't want to "rock the boat" and risk going through another long and traumatic period of mental illness. On the other hand, all treatments carry risks (e.g. medication side effects). We owe it to our patients to minimize the dosage required.

All effective treatments have the possibility of the patient experiencing negative side effects or a worsening of the condition. We always have to balance these risks with the benefits of treatment. This is true for any treatment that works (including behavioral treatment and psychotherapy) just as it is true for life. Do we totally avoid the experience of swimming in the sea because of a possible shark attack or do we analyze the actual odds of a shark attack on this particular beach? There is rarely potential benefit without taking risks. The best course is to carefully analyze the probable risks versus the possible benefits of any action we may plan to take.

People are usually more willing to face potential side effects of medications if this rationale of risk versus benefits is carefully explained. The medication risk can be put in perspective if it is compared to the risk of being hit by a car when crossing a road. We take precautions, we look both ways, and we go forward with both eyes open. Accidents still happen but most people proceed safely on their way to the other side.

There exists another form of risk. This is the risk of not treating a serious mental illness! Recent research on young people who are in the early stages of schizophrenia indicate that delaying treatment may result in a worse prognosis. There may even be more brain damage if the mental illness is left untreated.

THE FAMILIES
Secondary to the mental illness, and not the direct cause of it, is total family burn-out.

We know that there are many ways that families function with a child with a disability. For many (including some families in this book), the experience is not all negative. On the contrary, the experience of raising a child with ID has helped many families strengthen their values and beliefs about life. There has been a great deal of material written about the positive effects of having a child with Intellectual Disability. The fact remains, however, that most families of children with mental illness and/or challenging behaviors are much more likely to experience a poorer quality of life. It is these families who require specific dedicated supports once the additional mental health component has been identified.

It is unreasonable to expect ordinary people to cope with problems that even highly-experienced, specifically-trained medical professionals find challenging. Compound the emotional pressures with 24-hour, 365 days a year of extensive personal-care and it is easy to see why even the strongest, most loving parents can reach the point of exhaustion and defeat. Raising a child is a commitment for life. Children without ID or any physical problems can be challenging enough. Many marriages have trouble surviving childhood behavior problems, financial woes or long term illness of any nature. When families have the strength, integrity and commitment to work through all of these issues PLUS the added component of mental illness, they deserve recognition and the full support and understanding of the community. This support must be individualized as much as possible and must include counseling, financial assistance and adequate professional care. Any funding that helps to preserve the family unit and prevent total breakdown of the primary caregivers is money well-spent. Any funding that ensures appropriate and dedicated health care is money that inevitably saves future costs of social services down the road.

Information is the key to understanding. We hope this book will provide that information. We look forward to a new era of understanding. We, the clinicians, salute these families whose love and life-long dedication to their children is truly a testament to the wonder of the human spirit.

—RF

EDITOR'S NOTES

It probably would have been an easier task for each family to write a whole book. Most of them could have filled journals to chronicle all the stages of diagnosis, treatment, recovery and/or setbacks they experienced. It would take pages and pages to describe each problem, hurdle and fragile step they had to take from the beginning of their journey to where they are now. Multiple chapters would be needed just to vent about the frustrations of being at the mercy of burnt-out social workers, outdated government policies, inappropriate support services and, too often, seemingly callous medical practitioners. We asked these wonderful people to pare their thoughts to one chapter!

Some parents sent us packages of personal experiences with files and references attached. Others submitted brief notes highlighting one particular incident or memory. The job of editing was to find the core of each story. In some cases, the story was expanded; in others, the story had to be pared down for clarity and space restrictions. Names of hospitals and/or doctors were removed for legal reasons. Names of the majority of the people were changed to protect confidentiality.

Although the residual anger of some individuals could be appreciated, specific descriptions of confrontations with certain practitioners were deleted. Even with names being changed, the possibility of someone feeling they had been personally maligned, with no recourse for defense, had some risk. This book was not written as a platform for personal vendetta but as a testimony to the existence of dual diagnosis and the importance of recognizing that people with intellectual disabilities can also become mentally ill.

Each person on the face of the earth, at one time or other must face challenges. The problems for each individual vary in depth and scope. With the disabled, difficulties become multiplied as every single facet of their life is affected. Many people spend years in agony, their families suffering along with them, before it is realized that there are *two* problems manifesting in confusing symptoms. It takes a special team of dedicated professionals to diagnose the secondary illness. Far too often, neither recognition nor adequate funding is directed to the support of such specialization.

As I read, and then re-read, each submission, I couldn't help but become emotionally involved. It was a difficult task to leave some things out because there were some very interesting anecdotes. According to the contributors, there are just as many physicians that deserve to be publicly chastened as there are clinicians and support people that deserve to be publicly praised.

My job was to help the families compress their journey into one chapter, to organize details chronologically, to make cold facts more reader-friendly and to ensure that the most important details of their story were preserved.

Lest any reader feel that any portion of the book was edited without true understanding, it should be noted that one of the stories is from my own family. We have experienced the same heartaches and frustrations. We have also delighted in the same joys of little successes.

I thank all of the families and individuals who trusted me with their lives. I also thank Dr. Friedlander and Tina Donnelly for honoring me with the editing of this important project.

The book became a labor of love for all of us.

—*MH*

GLOSSARY

Acute Infantile Hemiplegia: Acute hemiplegia in childhood has many causes. Many are vascular, some follow trauma or encephalitis. Carotid and other basal vascular occlusions may result from cardiac emboli, angiomas, small vessel disease, or, in some cases, from an arteritis. Children may be left with significant motor deficits, hyperkinetic behavior, recurrent seizures and/or cognitive defects.

Aicardi Syndrome: Aicardi syndrome is a rare genetic disorder identified in 1965. The number of identified cases of children with Aicardi syndrome has been estimated at less than 500 worldwide.

Aicardi syndrome is characterized by:

a) Absence of the corpus callosum, either partial or complete (the corpus callosum is the part of the brain that sits between the right and left sides of the brain and allows the right side to communicate with the left.)

b) Infantile spasms (a form of seizures)

c) Lesions or "lacunae" of the retina of the eye very specific to this disorder

d) Other lesions of the brain such as microcephaly, (small brain); enlarged ventricles; or porencephalic cysts (a gap in the brain where there should be healthy brain tissue)

Aicardi syndrome only affects females, and in very rare cases, males with Klinefelter syndrome (XXY). Children are most commonly identified with Aicardi Syndrome before the age of five months. A significant number of these girls are products of normal births and seem to be developing normally until around the age of three months, when they begin to have infantile spasms. The known age range of affected children is from birth to the late forties. (Credit: Aicardi Syndrome foundation, www.aicardisyndrome.org

Alfies Syndrome: (Deletion q9 Syndrome). This syndrome is a chromosomal disorder with characteristics including a mean IQ of 49, cranial formation abnormalities, prominent eyes, highly arched eyebrows, small mouth, short neck, low hairline, long slender fingers and toes, foot positioning defects, scoliosis (abnormal curvature of the spine), and hernia (Jones, Kenneth Lyons, M.D. 1997. *Smith's Recognizable Patterns of Human Malformation.* W.B. Saunders Co. Philadelphia, P.A.).

Alzheimer's disease: A dementia characterized by the development of multiple cognitive deficits of memory, language disturbance, motor activity impairment, failure to recognize objects and disturbance in executive functioning (planning, organizing, sequencing, abstracting). These issues cause impairment in social and/or occupational functioning. Onset is gradual and there is a continuing cognitive decline. Cognitive deficits are not due to other central nervous system conditions, systemic conditions, substance-induced condition or Axis I mental illness. (American Psychiatric Association, 2000, Diagnostic Criteria from DSM-IV-TR, Arlington, VA).

Anafranil: Anafranil (Clomipramine) is a tricyclic medication with antidepressant and antiobsessional properties. Used mostly for treatment of obsessive compulsive behaviors in OCD and autism. Possible side effects are dry mouth, urinary retention; blurred vision, constipation, drowsiness, dizziness, orthostatic hypotension, tachycardia and weight gain (Ralph, Irene. 2006. *Psychotropic Agents* 14th *Edition,* IGR Publications. Grand Forks, B.C., Canada).

Asperger's Syndrome: Asperger's syndrome is demonstrated by 1) qualitative impairment in social interaction, 2) restricted repetitive and stereotyped patterns of behavior, interests and activities and 3) clinically significant impairment in social, occupational, or other areas of functioning. There is no significant delay in language or cognitive development as is found in more classic forms of Autism (American Psychiatric Association 2000, *Diagnostic Criteria from DSM—IV-TR*, Arlington, VA).

Autism: Autism is demonstrated by 1) qualitative impairment in social interaction, 2) qualitative impairments in communication and 3) restricted repetitive and stereotyped patterns of behavior. There are delays or abnormal functioning in at least one of the following: 1) social interaction, 2) language as used in social communication and/or 3) symbolic or imaginative play (American Psychiatric Association. 2000, *Diagnostic Criteria from DSM-IV-TR*, Arlington, VA).

Bipolar Mood Disorder: (Manic Depression) is characterized by episodes of disturbed mood and activity level. These episodes consist of switches from an elevation of mood and increased energy and activity (mania) to a lowering of mood and decreased energy and activity (depression). Manic episodes begin abruptly and last for two weeks to five months. Depressions last approximately six months (World Health Organization. 1996. Multiaxial Classification of Child and Adolescent Psychiatric Disorders, Cambridge University Press. Cambridge, UK).

Candida: Candida is a genus of yeast-like imperfect fungi, commonly part of the normal flora of the mouth, skin, intestinal tract and vagina, but can cause a variety of infections, including thrush and vaginitis (W.B. Saunders Co. 1988. 27th Dorland's Illustrated Medical Dictionary. Philadelphia, P.A.).

CBI: (Communication Behavior Instruction) CBI Consultants is an agency based out of Vancouver B.C. that provides training, consulting and research in the area of behavioral support for individuals with developmental disabilities (info@cbiconsultants.com).

Cerebral Palsy: CP is a group of nonprogressive syndromes causing motor impairment secondary to lesions or anomalies of the brain occurring during brain development. Muscle tone impairment may range from spasticity to hypo tonicity (Rubin, L.R., MD & Crocker, A.C., MD. 2006. *Medical Care for Children & Adults with Developmental Disabilities,* Paul H Brookes Publishing. Baltimore, Maryland).

Clonazepam: This medication is an anxiolytic benzodiazepine used to treat acute anxiety. Use should be limited to several weeks to a few months to avoid dependence. Possible side effects may be drowsiness, confusion, paradoxical excitement or dizziness (Ralph, Irene. 2006. Psychotropic Agents 14th Edition 2006. IGR Publications, Grand Forks, B.C.).

Clozapine: Clozapine is a very effective novel antipsychotic medication used to treat schizophrenia and other psychotic disorders. Possible side effects that may occur are weight gain, decreased libido, sedation dizziness, confusion or agranulocytosis (blood disorder that can lead to life threatening infection) (Ralph, Irene. 2006. *Psychotropic agents* 14th Edition 2006. IGR Publications, Grand Forks B.C.).

Community Living British Columbia: CLBC is a government funded Crown Corporation in BC whose mandate is to support individuals with developmental disabilities to live fully integrated lives as citizens in our society (www.communitylivingbc.ca).

Cornelia De Lange Syndrome: (Duplication 3q Syndrome) is a chromosomal disorder resulting in abnormalities such as severe postnatal growth deficiency, severe mental deficiency with brain anomalies/seizures, abnormal head shape, cleft palate, malformed ears, webbed neck and cardiac and/or renal defects (Jones, K.L., MD. 1997. Smith's Recognizable Patterns of Human Malformation. W.B. Saunders Co. Philadelphia, PA).

DD: (Developmental Disability) DD is a term used in BC to refer to children and adults with significantly sub average intellectual functioning: an IQ of approximately 70 or below , onset before the age of eighteen years and concurrent deficits in adaptive functioning in at least two of the following areas: communication, self care, home living, social/interpersonal skills, use of community resources, self-direction, functional academic skills, work leisure, health and safety (American Psychiatric Association. 2000, *Diagnostic Criteria from DSM_IV_TR,* Arlington, VA). In some provinces or countries, DD is referred to as Mental Retardation, Intellectual Disability (ID) or Mental Handicap.

We prefer the term ID.

Depo-Provera: This medication is a long acting injectable form of birth control made of progestogen derived from a natural source (soybeans). Some potential side effects are irregular menses, weight gain, headache and abdominal discomfort (Canadian Pharmacists Association. 2005. Compendium of Pharmaceuticals and Specialties. Ottawa, ON).

Depression: Major Depressive Disorder is a mental health disorder characterized by distinct episodes of depression lasting for at least 2 weeks in duration and including other symptoms such as sleep and/or appetite disturbance, weight changes, loss of pleasure, feelings of hopelessness, loss of libido, feelings of guilt and worthlessness and thoughts of death and/or suicide (American Psychiatric Association. 2000, *Diagnostic Criteria from DSM_IV_TR.* Arlington, VA).

Divalproex: (Epival in Canada and Depakote in the USA) is a mood stabilizer used in the treatment of bipolar disorder, as well as an anticonvulsant used in the treatment of seizure disorders. Some possible side effects are liver dysfunction, rash, headache, abdominal pain, gastric complaints, dizziness and tremor (Canadian Pharmacists Association. 2005. *Compendium of Pharmaceuticals and Specialties.* Ottawa, ON).

Down Syndrome: DS is a chromosomal disorder occurring in 1 in 700 live births. Some features of DS are intellectual impairment, flat facial profile, small skin folds at the inner corner of the eyes, increased incidence of heart defects, poor muscle tone, short stature, large tongue and language difficulties (Hopkins, Brian. 2005, *The Cambridge Encyclopedia of Child Development,* Cambridge, UK).

Effexor (Venlafaxine): This is a medication used primarily for treatment of depressive and anxiety disorders. Some potential side effects are nausea, vomiting, increased sweating, constipation, increase in blood pressure and headache (Ralph, Irene, 2006, *Psychotropic Agents* 14th Edition 2006. IGR Publications, Grand Forks, B.C.).

Epilepsy: This is a medical condition characterized by seizures that are a result of abnormal brain activity. The prevalence in the general population is 0.7%-1%, and in individuals with an IQ below 70 it is 5%-10% Rubin, L.I., MD & Crocker, A.C., MD. 2006. Medical Care for Children & Adults with Developmental Disabilities. Brookes Publishing Co. Baltimore, Maryland).

Epival: See Divalproex

Fluvoxamine: (Luvox) is an antidepressant medication commonly used to treat depressive disorder, panic disorder and/or anxiety. Some potential side effects are nausea, dry mouth, headache, sedation, dizziness, sweating and sexual side effects (Ralph, Irene. 2006. Psychotropic Agents 14th Edition 2006. IGR Publications, Grand Forks, B.C.).

Gabapentan: (Neurontin) is a mood stabilizer and anticonvulsant medication. It has anti-anxiety and anti-agitation effects and few side effects. Potential side effects that may occur are fatigue, weight gain, digestive complaints, dizziness and tremor (Canadian Pharmacists Association. 2005. Compendium of Pharmaceuticals and Specialties. Ottawa, ON).

Grand Mal seizures: also called a generalized tonic-clonic seizure. This refers to an episode of altered or loss of consciousness lasting generally 1- 3 minutes in duration. The tonic phase consists of a sustained increase in muscle contraction lasting a few seconds to minutes and is followed by a clonic phase consisting of sudden, brief involuntary contractions of muscles or muscle groups (Rubin, L.I., MD & Crocker, A.C., MD. 2006. *Medical Care for Children & Adults with Developmental Disabilities.* Paul H Brookes Publishing Co. Baltimore, Maryland).

Haloperidol: (Haldol) is a first generation antipsychotic medication used to treat schizophrenia, other psychotic disorders and autism. Some possible side effects are stiffness, tremor, drooling, weakness, fatigue, restlessness, facial grimacing, high fever and confusion (Ralph, Irene. 2006. *Psychotropic Agents* 14th Edition 2006, IGR Publications, Grand Forks, B.C.).

Hyperactivity: Pervasive and severe over activity is a core symptom of Attention Deficit Hyperactivity Disorder (ADHD).

ID: Intellectual Disability (See Developmental Disability).

IDMH: Intellectual Disability with Mental Health Disorder (also called Dual Diagnosis).

Infant Febrile seizures: This type of seizure occurs in infants due to a sustained elevation in body temperature (Rubin, L.I. & Crocker, AC, 2006. *Medical Care for Children & Adults with Developmental Disabilities,* Paul H Brookes Publishing Co.).

Lamictal: (Lamotrigine) is a mood stabilizer and anticonvulsant medication used to treat bipolar depression and/or seizure disorder. Some potential side effects are confusion, dizziness, gastric distress, blurred vision and fever (Ralph, Irene. 2006. *Psychotropic Agents* 14th Edition 2006. IGR Publications, Grand Forks, B.C.).

Metformin: (Glucophage) is a medication for diabetes used to stabilize elevated blood sugar. Some potential side effects are lactic acidosis, gastrointestinal symptoms, metallic taste and skin rash (Canadian Pharmacists Association. 2005. Compendium of Pharmaceuticals and Specialties. Ottawa, ON).

NADD: (The National Association for the Dually Diagnosed) is an association for persons with developmental disabilities and mental health needs in North America. It provides professionals, educators, policy makers, and families with information on mental health issues relating to people with intellectual or developmental disabilities (info@thenadd.org).

Neurologist: A physician who specializes in disorders of the brain, such as seizures.

NMS: (Neuroleptic Malignancy Syndrome) is a rare potentially fatal adverse effect of antipsychotic medication. Symptoms of the syndrome include unusually high fever, muscular rigidity, convulsions, sweating, increased heartbeat, weakness, confusion, fast breathing, agitation and pallor (Ralph, Irene. 2006. Psychotropic Agents 14th Edition 2006. IGR Publications, Grand Forks, B.C.).

Nortripyline: (Aventyl) is a tricyclic antidepressant medication used for depression, anxiety, insomnia and pain management (Ralph, Irene. 2006. *Psychotropic Agents* 14th Edition 2006. IGR Publications, Grand Forks, B.C.).

NOS: (Not Otherwise Specified) used a suffix to refer to clusters of atypical symptoms of mental illness.

Novo-glybride: (Sulfonylureas) is a medication used to stabilize blood sugar in type II diabetes. Some possible side effects are low blood sugar, weight gain, skin rash, nausea, heartburn and jaundice (Canadian Pharmacists Association. 2005. *Compendium of Pharmaceuticals and Specialties.* Ottawa, ON.).

OCD: (Obsessive Compulsive Disorder) is an anxiety disorder characterized by repetitive thoughts (obsessions) and compulsive actions, e.g., excessive hand washing, hoarding. (World Health Organization 1996 *Multiaxial Classification of Child and Adolescent Psychiatric Disorders,* Cambridge University Press. Cambridge, UK).

Olanzepine: (Zyprexa) is second generation antipsychotic medication used in the treatment of psychotic and mood disorders. Some potential side effects are dizziness, dry mouth, weight gain, fluid retention, agitation, nausea and vomiting (Ralph, Irene. 2006. *Psychotropic Agents* 14th Edition 2006. IGR Publications, Grand Forks, B.C.).

Paranoia: Paranoia can be a feature of a psychotic disorder; for example the development of delusions whereby the individual is fearful of a situation not based in reality, e.g., that other people are pursuing him/her (World Health Organization. 1996. *Multiaxial Classification of Child and Adolescent Psychiatric Disorders.* Cambridge University Press, Cambridge, UK).

Paxil: (Paroxetine) is an antidepressant medication used in the treatment of depression, obsessive-compulsive disorder, panic disorder and social anxiety disorder. Some potential side effects are weight gain, nausea, sexual problems, nausea and headache (Ralph, Irene. 2006. Psychotropic Agents 14th Edition 2006. IGR Publications, Grand Forks, B.C.).

Petit Mal seizures: This is a type of seizure where there is a sudden momentary loss of consciousness with only minor muscular contractions (W.B. Saunders Co. 1988. *Dorlands Illustrated Medical Dictionary.* Philadelphia, PA).

Phenobarbital: This medication is rarely used nowadays. It is classified as a "barbiturate." It may be used as an anticonvulsant, sedative and/or hypnotic. Some possible side effects are dependence, drowsiness, low blood pressure, facial swelling and skin rash (Canadian Pharmacists Association. 2005. Compendium of Pharmaceuticals and Specialties. Ottawa, ON).

Phobia: This is a phenomenon where anxiety is evoked by certain well-defined situations or objects that are not currently dangerous,

e.g., fear of small spaces or fear of animals (World Health Organization. 1996. *Multiaxial Classification of Child and Adolescent Psychiatric Disorders*, Cambridge University Press. Cambridge, UK.

Prozac: (Fluoxetine) is an antidepressant medication used to treat
depression, obsessive-compulsive disorder, bulimia, panic disorder
and social anxiety disorder. Some possible side effects are nausea, agitation, insomnia, mania, rash and fever (Ralph, Irene. 2006.
Psychotropic Agents 14th Edition 2006. IGR Publications, Grand
Forks, B.C.).

Psychiatrist: A doctor practicing the field of Psychiatry. Psychiatry is a
medical specialty dealing with the prevention, assessment, diagnosis,
treatment, and rehabilitation of mental illness such as clinical depression, bipolar disorder, schizophrenia and anxiety disorders. Its primary goal is the relief of mental suffering and improvement of
mental well-being. Diagnostic assessment of the person is via a biological, psychological, and social/cultural perspective. An illness or
problem can then be managed by medication various forms of psychotherapy or behavioral therapy and/or changes in the environment. The word 'psychiatry' derives from the Green for "healer of
the spirit". (www.en.wikepdia.org)

Psychologist: A specialist who can talk with patients and their families
about emotional and personal matters, and can help them make decisions.

They are trained and educated to perform psychological
research, testing, and therapy.

Psychosis: This is a category of mental disorder characterized by gross
impairment in reality testing evidenced by delusions, hallucinations,
incoherent speech, or disorganized behavior without awareness on

the part of the person that the behavior is abnormal (W.B. Saunders Co. 1988. *Dorland's Illustrated Medical Dictionary*. Philadelphia, PA).

Psychosocial: This pertains to the "psycho" (state of the mind) and social (environmental) aspects of the individual (W.B. Saunders Co. 1988. *Dorlands Illustrated Medical Dictionary*. Philadelphia, PA).

Risperidol (Also: Risperdal): RISPERDAL® (risperidone) is a second generation antipsychotic medication which is indicated for schizophrenia and to treat the manic symptoms of acute manic or mixed episodes associated with Bipolar I Disorder.(Credit: Janssen). It is also widely used in North America to improve behavioral symptoms associated with autism.

Rubella Syndrome: Prior to the introduction of the rubella vaccine, rubella infection of the fetus in pregnancy caused significant morbidity and mortality. Some of the effects include cataracts, blindness, sensory hearing loss, behavior disorders and intellectual disability (Rubin, L.I., MD & Crocker, A.C., MD. 2006. *Medical Care for Children and Adults with Developmental Disabilities,* Paul H Brookes Publishing. Baltimore, Maryland).

Schizophrenia: Schizophrenic disorders are a form of psychosis and are manifested by distortions in thinking and perception and by inappropriate or blunted expression of mood. Hallucinations are common, particularly auditory. Delusions (false, fixed beliefs not based on reality) may occur. Speech may be incoherent and the ability to carry out the activities of daily living may regress (World Health Organization. 1996. *Multiaxial Classification of Child and Adolescent Psychiatric Disorders,* Cambridge University Press, Cambridge Press).

Scoliosis: This is an appreciable lateral deviation of the normally straight vertical line of the spine (W.B. Saunders Co. 1988. *Dorland's Illustrated Medical Dictionary.* Philadelphia, PA).

Seroquel: (Quetiapine) is a second generation antipsychotic medication used for the treatment of schizophrenia and other psychotic disorders. Some side effects that may be experienced are constipation, lowered blood pressure, weight gain, headache and agitation (Ralph, Irene. 2006. Psychotropic Medications 14th Edition 2006. IGR Publications, Grand Forks, B.C.)

Syndrome: A term used to refer to a collection of symptoms and signs of a disease which occur together more than by chance.

Tardive Dyskinesa: TD is an involuntary movement disorder which may appear with long term treatment with antipsychotic medications. Some signs of the disorder are backward-forward curling of the tongue, chewing movements, facial grimacing, twisting/turning of the shoulders and hips, difficulty swallowing, and awkward gait (Ralph, Irene. 2006. Psychotropic Agents 14th Edition 2006. IGR Publications, Grand Forks, B.C.).

Tegretol: (Carbamazepine) is an anticonvulsant medication used for the treatment of seizure disorder and bipolar disorder. Potential side effects may be drowsiness, dizziness, confusion, fatigue, anemia, rash, lowered blood pressure and nausea (Ralph, Irene. 2006. Psychotropic Agents 14th Edition 2006. IGR Publications, Grand Forks, B.C.).

Topomax: Topiramate (brand name: Topamax®) is an anticonvulsant drug produced byOrtho-McNeil, a division of Johnson & Johnson. It is used to treat epilepsy in both children and adults. In children it is also indicated for treatment of Lennox-Gastaut syndrome (a disorder that causes seizures and developmental delays). It is also Food and Drug Administration(FDA) approved for, and now most frequently prescribed for, the prevention of migraines. It has been used by psychiatrists to treat bipolar disorder, although it is not FDA approved for this purpose and such use is somewhat controversial. A pilot study suggests that Topiramate is possibly effective against infantile spasm. (Credit: Wikipedia: www.en.wikepedia.org)

Tuberous Sclerosis: This is a genetic disorder that can affect any organ system with the growth of benign tumors, that most often affect the brain, heart, skin lungs, eyes and kidneys. It can lead to seizures, intellectual disabilities, autism and fatal heart, lung or kidney disease (Rubin, L.I., MD & Crocker, A.C., MD. 2006. Medical Care for Children and Adults with Developmental Disabilities. Paul H Brookes Publishing Co. Baltimore, Maryland).

Undifferentiated Schizophrenia: (See schizophrenia) this condition meets the general diagnostic criteria for schizophrenia, but does not conform to any one subtype, or exhibits the features of more than one of the subtypes (World Health Organization. 1996. Multiaxial Classification of Child and Adolescent Psychiatric Disorders, Cambridge University Press. Cambridge, UK).

Williams Syndrome: This is a genetic disorder characterized by features such as a broad forehead, flat nasal bridge, fleshy lips, prominent ears, curly hair, heart defects, visual and hearing impairments, short stature and intellectual disability. Language skills are typically much more advanced than in other individuals with similar IQ (Rubin, I.L., MD & Crocker, A.C., MD 2006. *Medical Care for Children and Adults with Developmental Disabilities.* Paul H Brookes Publishing Co. Baltimore, Maryland).

ROBIN FRIEDLANDER

Robin Friedlander is a psychiatrist and a Clinical Associate Professor at the University of British Columbia. He works in the Neuropsychiatry Clinic at BC Children's Hospital in Vancouver, BC, treating children with neuro-developmental disorders and their families.

Dr. Friedlander is also Clinical Director of the West Coast & Fraser Valley Mental Health Support Teams, a group which provides specialized community-based mental health treatment for adolescents and adults with Developmental Disabilities (DD) in the Lower Mainland of BC.

Born and educated in South Africa, he is married with two adolescent boys.

TINA DONNELLY, RPN, BHSC

After earning her registration, Tina practiced psychiatric nursing in the Woodlands Residential Facility, New Westminster, BC for nineteen years, and then transferred to the practice of community mental health. She completed her Bachelor of Health Science in Psychiatric Nursing degree while working in her chosen field. Personal experience with a family member directed her interest and energies towards people diagnosed with intellectual disabilities, and her career became focused in this area. For the past ten years she has managed two community health teams in the Lower Mainland of British Columbia which specialize and provide both mental health and behavioral services to people with intellectual disabilities and mental illness.

Her philosophy emphasizes the utilization of a multimodal treatment approach which incorporates a wide variety of professionals, including psychiatrists, psychologists, nurses, behavior therapists, art therapists, specialized counselors and sexuality educators/ consultants. Within this framework, and with strong family and/or caregiver support ensuring the continuity of treatment plans, individuals often show real progress and it is this pattern of relative success that gives Tina great satisfaction.

Tina will continue to be a strong advocate for community inclusion and she hopes that this book will give its readers a better understanding of those who are experiencing intellectual disabilities.

MADELINE HOMBERT

Madeline Hombert writes for newspapers and magazines as well as for film. Two of her screenplay collaborations have been produced as feature films and a third is in development.

Most recently, she has added editing to her credits. A favorite book project, *Who's Got The Ring*, for author Nomi Whalen, is distributed through Amazon and Chapters.

Madeline is married and the mother of three. (One deceased). Nominated as a YWCA "Woman of Distinction," Madeline remains active in her community.

RIIA TALVE (artist)

The cover art was provided by Riia Talve, a young artist from Delta, British Columbia. More of Riia's work is found in the chapter dedicated to her.

Ms. Talve is a student of the Emily Carr Institute of Art & Design in Vancouver. Her work has been acknowledged and praised by such internationally-renowned artists as Robert Bateman and her paintings are found in many private and corporate collections. (www.rtalve.com)

All photographs in this book were produced by Hari Panesar, Tijrah Photography, Delta, BC.